HOW TO TALK
WITH PEOPLE

HOW TO TALK WITH PEOPLE

*A Program for Preventing Troubles
That Come When People
Talk Together*

by Irving J. Lee

The School of Speech, Northwestern University

International Society for General Semantics
San Francisco

INTERNATIONAL SOCIETY
FOR GENERAL SEMANTICS

Post Office Box 2469 • San Francisco, California 94126

Library of Congress catalog card number: 52-5459
ISBN 0-918970-30-X

To
David Alfred

Contents

Foreword

This is a time of much talk.

It would be hard to estimate how helpful it is or how destructive. Of this we may be sure: without the means, the capacity, and the will to communicate, what we know as business, government, and community activities could not be. Indeed, even in 1952 men around the world wait nervously to see whether the East and West can find ways of talking together before the bombs fall.

That communication between men is a significant phenomenon need hardly be argued. It is more than a straw in the wind when the National Association of Manufacturers, the editors of *Fortune,* and professors of philosophy in the universities become explicit in their interest in language and communication. The mounting output of workers in the fields of speech, general semantics, group dynamics, and non-directive counseling is testimony that the phenomena of discussion are being studied now as never before.

From Talking At to Talking With

For fifteen years in public speaking classes I have been encouraging people to talk to others. In that time

I have listened to thousands of talks—describing, pleading, condemning. Sometimes the talk came from earnest reflection, sometimes from a digest magazine. In either case, the performance did something for the student. His perspiration paid off in the form of an achievement that both he and his audience could recognize. He learned to talk steadily in spite of his fearfulness. He caught the feeling of power that comes when one affects another. Every now and then someone moved to the rostrum with that eagerness which says, "Listen, this is my idea." Many were stirred by their own persuasion to study and think some more.

Even though there were values in those class exercises, I became aware that something was amiss.

The précis assignment was invariably troublesome. Each listener would be asked to write in his own words a fifty-word abstract or summary of what a speaker said. Only rarely would the speaker (after study of the abstracts) report that more than 25 percent of the class adequately "got it." They reported something but it was not "his idea as he gave it." If the audience heard they did not seem to listen. Or if they listened, it seemed with half an ear.

The open-forum question periods were often unsatisfactory, too. Listeners went off on tangents. They picked up incidental items and drew from them conclusions that could be warranted only if the speaker had not given the rest of his speech.

Then there were the crises when a dearly held belief was dismissed with the implication that the holder was only one or two steps removed from idiocy. If these moments of drama turned on matters of religion and politics, the speaking took fire almost in inverse ratio to the thinness of the argumentative fuel. The problem then was to find ways of preventing everyone from talking all at once. But there was little in these exchanges which showed a desire to talk together. It was as if each felt that if only he had his say somehow everything would clear up.

After such rounds of high talk, we would try the "issues game." This was an attempt to have the issues and points of difference stated so that the contending parties might face them together. Over and over in these classes this was the beginning of a new ruckus. The very effort to describe what the argument was about set off new arguments. Each person "knew" what he was talking about and little did he care about the other fellow—except to point out that none was making the effort to hear *him* out.

It dawned on me ever so slowly that it was not enough merely to encourage people to talk *to* others. They needed to know how to talk *with* others, too. I am not saying that there is no place for the promotion of skill in partisan speech-making. I am saying that, along with it, people need the art of human communion with each other.

What happens to discussions in the little world of the classroom is hardly important. The same obstruc tionist attitudes in the talk situation outside, however, might waste time, cost money, and intensify confusion and conflict. When foremen and workers, physicians and patients, officers and enlisted men, sales managers and salesmen, management and union representatives, members of boards and committees talk together in ways which end in trouble, these attitudes make a difference.

But what actually happens in such groups and what can be done about it? Professor J. H. McBurney had offered his pioneering course at Northwestern University and with Professor K. G. Hance had written the ground-breaking textbook, *The Principles and Methods of Discussion*. I had been exposed to both. I had read much of what Lyman Bryson, Harrison S. Elliott, Mary Follett, Eduard Lindeman, Alfred Dwight Sheffield, John W. Studebaker, Ordway Tead had written about the group process. I found the writings of Elton Mayo, C. I. Barnard, and F. J. Roethlisberger rewarding. But they all seemed to be on an instructional level once removed from what I wanted. They seemed to stop just short of the details I wanted to know more about. I began a catalogue of the varieties of communication breakdown in my classes. I found a perspective and hints of what to look for in Alfred Korzybski's formulations of general semantics. I began to take notes on things that happened in committee meetings I attended. There were recurring strains and themes. Would they be found beyond the campus?

Since 1942 I have listened to and taken notes on the deliberations of more than 200 groups. Some 150 of these were staff, board, and committee meetings in private businesses, military organizations, and community agencies. The remaining were in and around the university. These were not learning sessions but occasions where policies and plans had to be made and modes of action worked out. These were "real" situations.

The pages that follow describe some of the things I saw and heard and a number of the corrective measures that worked in varying degrees of success in some of the groups willing to experiment. I had help from many secretaries writing minutes, and from stenographers whose shorthand was better than mine. Occasionally a tape recorder was available and good use was made of it. One regrets that there weren't more such recordings. Only occasionally do I give illustrations from the meetings I attended. It seems to me that a visitor or participant has no license to make a public analysis of what he was privileged to see and hear. That is also the reason why the organizations remain anonymous and why fictitious names are used throughout. I regret this device because I should have liked to pay my public respects to those men and women who both permitted and suffered my presence and so generously endured my interviewing. And to those observers who didn't always think that they were spending their time usefully.

It seems necessary to say that what is presented here gives few final answers. Indeed, those given are given without the assurance that they will similarly apply elsewhere. The first person was permitted entry as a way of emphasizing the restricted character and scope of the findings, and not, it is hoped, as a means of giving the findings a privileged status.

There is much in the observational procedures which is less than rigorous. Checks on the reliability of the observations were only occasionally possible. What is said here may be considered the output of one making a time-and-motion study in a situation which could not be repeated. Perhaps the very lack of controls and precision in what is here presented may encourage others to fill in what is required.

I am glad to acknowledge the editorial assistance I received from Mr. Robert R. Hume of the Northwestern University Traffic Institute and the criticisms of Mr. Victor M. Ratner, vice-president of Macy's. I wish it had been possible for me to incorporate more of their suggestions.

I must record here my indebtedness to two men who died before the manuscript was completed. Both are involved in the letter and spirit of my writing. Dr. James M. Yard helped me immeasurably in the planning and arranging of the research. Alfred Korzybski's role in my preparation for this kind of study is equally immeasurable.

IRVING J. LEE

February, 1952

HOW TO TALK WITH PEOPLE

CHAPTER I

A Preview of the Problem

Effective coöperation, then, is the problem we face in the middle period of the twentieth century. There is no "ism" that will help us to solution; we must be content to return to patient, pedestrian work at the wholly neglected problem of the determinants of spontaneous participation. —Elton Mayo, *The Social Problems of an Industrial Civilization*, Harvard University, Graduate School of Business Administration, 1945, p. xvi.

There are disasters we seem unable to do much about—earthquakes, tornadoes, the proliferation of cells in cancer.

There are calamities we seem to contribute to—fires, collisions, housing shortages.

And then there are troubles we seem to create—disagreements and conflicts which run the range from name-calling to war.

The terrors of nature are being fought with courage

and ingenuity. We approach those that are man-made with less assurance. Maybe the human problems are so big and so numerous that fumbling is inevitable. Maybe those interested in the improvement of human relations have been frightened by the magnitude of what they face. Whatever the reason, this is hardly the time for despair. Though we do not find solutions there may be value in our looking anew at the varieties of human disturbance. From that perspective we might find the courage to keep trying whatever means we have.

In this book I report an attempt to look at some human troubles—those that come when men and women talk together. The committee room is far from being the most important scene of human interaction. It is, however, convenient and confined. In it one can see on a reduced scale the way conflicts begin and go on.

Three questions interested me: (1) Do people make an effort to understand each other? (2) How do they respond when another talks? (3) How do they approach problems?

Many other questions were asked. But those were the ones I found some answers for. And in connection with the difficulties that were thus defined, we were able to try out some suggestions for analysis, prevention, and correction.

So as to indicate something of the scope and character of what is involved in this interest, the major findings and suggestions are here summarized.

1. Misunderstanding results when one man assumes that another uses words just as *he* does. People are so eager to reply that they rarely do enough inquiring. They believe so surely (and wrongly) that words have meaning in themselves that they hardly ever wonder what the speaker means when he uses them.

Suggestion: Committee members need exercises in listening. They must learn not how to define terms but how to ask others what they are intending to say. Our advice: Don't blame the speaker alone for the misunderstanding. The listener is involved, too. It takes two to make communication.

2. Trouble comes when somebody contradicts somebody else without seeing what the first man was talking about. The speaker says, "You can't trust the Abibs." The listener says, "Yes, you can." Then they go at it. When the speaker was asked to specify, he told about Samo and Har and Myri. And, of course, they were untrustworthy. When the listener specified, he told about Mil and Janx and Car. And without a doubt they could be trusted. If the contradictor had asked first, the contradictee might not have had his feelings hurt. And the committee might have come to conclusions without that waste of time. The trouble mounts when nobody bothers about specifying.

Suggestion: Both leaders and members need to learn how to spot temperature-raising contradictions. They must ask, ever so politely: Are you differing on the details or on the conclusion? Does your generalization refer to what his does?

3. The most frequently bothersome kind of disagreement arises when someone assumes this: "If his feeling about it is different from mine, he has no good reason for feeling so." It is then a short step to this: "If he doesn't see it my way, he is a fool." What is important here is not that men disagree, but that they become disagreeable about it.

Suggestion: What should a leader do about a person who is suspicious and impatient in the presence of those who differ with him? First, he must realize that his job is not to prevent differences in judgment but to get at the assumption that if-he-has-ideas-at-variance-with-mine-then-he-necessarily-doesn't-know-what-he-is-talking-about. Second, he might arrange for the group's consideration of the nature of the disagreement process as a way of creating a common front against the steam-roller tactics of the arrogant member.

4. Going off on tangents is assisted, partisanship is encouraged, and time is wasted when a group is more interested in prescribing for problems than in describing them. Too often members of a group are willing

to fight about the answers even before they have explored the question.

Suggestion: The leader must be trained in the role of "prodder," so that he will do everything possible to keep the group problem-centered rather than solution-minded. He prods them with "What is it that has gone wrong?" even though they prefer "What should we do about it?"

5. To solve problems when everyone is of a like mind about the problems is hard enough. When a group is composed of some who look at problems as if they were just like those they solved before, and others who see the problems as if they were brand new and different—then one more difficulty is superimposed on the group.

Suggestion: Let the leader approach the business of the meeting in case fashion. No conclusions or recommendations are to be made until after the problem is presented in narrative form. The old-new controversy is thus kept in abeyance.

6. The deepest sort of conflict occurs when partisans meet head on, when each seeks to satisfy his or his organization's needs regardless of the needs of others. The leader's task is this: to see that each is satisfied without disrupting operations.

Suggestion: Someone should say something about the values of compromise. Too many well-meaning people have belittled this technique of settling disputes. But are stalemates and bitter battles to the end preferable? The leader may cleanse the atmosphere if he can be persuaded to affirm directly that there is decency in "giving a little" and intelligence in the desire "to work things out."

7. It is impossible to talk about men or ideas without naming them. But a name which has a stigmatizing effect can stop or deter sensible analysis. Stigma names hurt feelings and usually lead to more of the same.

Suggestion: The leader must not try to stop the name-calling. He should try to get participants to look beyond the limiting effects of the label. To keep the talk on the issue, not the name, he asks, "Is it that *only?* Does that name cover all of it?"

8. Conflict within a group is compounded when one person takes another's difference of opinion as a personal attack on himself. So many people seem not to realize that it is possible to quarrel on an issue without necessarily doubting another's sincerity or casting aspersions on his integrity.

Suggestion: To ward off the feeling of defensiveness which accompanies the "taking" of criticism, committee participants should be instructed in the use of a non-combative approach. This involves an effort on the part of a critic to soften the blow by disclaiming any attempt to manifest his superiority. He reassures his "opponent" that the issue alone is the objective.

9. A group faces a crisis the moment one person gets angry at another. Sometimes it blows over; sometimes it blows up. Angry men work against and not with each other.

Suggestion: What should a leader do then? Our advice: Do not try to deal with a man's emotional expression as such. Do not tell him to inhibit these responses. Do try to shift his attention to what it was that set him off. Do ask him to consider whether he is surmising as if he knew. Do urge him to take one more look at the object of his anger. The object is to re-align his perception so that he will think and feel anew.

10. In sixteen groups we saw illustrations of men and women talking together, spontaneously, coöperatively, constructively. There was team-play and team-work. We tried to isolate some of the factors we found there: (1) The leader did not try to tell the others what to do or how to think; he was thinking along with them. (2) No one presumed to know it all; one might be eager and vigorous in his manner of

talking, but he was amenable and attentive when others spoke. (3) The people thought of the accomplishments of the group rather than of their individual exploits.

Suggestion: To achieve some of this spontaneous togetherness, let a leader try the non-monitoring role. Then let a group take time off to talk about the values of the non-allness attitude and the non-solo sort of performance.

11. A leader sometimes gets so tired and discouraged when committee discussions drag on or bog down that he takes over the assignments himself. There is real trouble if he forgets that, instead of things adding up, they often pile up. It is then harder to talk to him. His assistants lose initiative. He becomes difficult to work with.

Suggestion: The chairman must be helped to face the fact that, if he does alone what a committee ought to help him with, he may not be adding to his burdens but disastrously complicating them. He needs to see that it may well be wise to give up rather than to take on responsibility. In addition, the group must be protected from overloading. "Analysis of the Agenda" might well be made the first order of business.

12. Under pressure to get things done a group is often willing to settle for some easy and inadequate

solution. That means that the trouble is postponed, not dissolved. Often, too, a busy executive, seeing that meetings take the time of well-paid personnel, tries to cut costs by urging them to deal with problems according to the clock rather than the complexity. This is a false economy which leads to cutting down on communication as if it did not have its own productive values.

Suggestion: When men succumb to the pressures of temporal efficiency they need to be helped to see the difference between *time-wasted* and *time-spent.* Human intelligence and imagination are not readily geared to the demands of a timepiece. When problems are big a group may need comparably big amounts of time.

13. Too many leaders work on, rather than work with, their members. They want meetings to be as workmanlike as a belt line. Because they take a business-only attitude, they expect the same from everybody else. They forget that people like to get things off their chests almost as much as they like to solve problems. They forget that meetings ought to be pleasant as well as productive.

Suggestion: If people in a group want to interrupt serious discussion with some diversion or personal expression—let them. Then bring them back to the agenda. Committees work best when the talk swings between the personal and the purposeful.

14. We found very few leaders who could handle their many responsibilities with equal effectiveness. When a man or woman had to act as organizer, clarifier, pacifier, and contributor, he had too much to do. He needed help.

Suggestion: Find someone in the group to take over the job of "reminder." This involves assisting the chairman in noting and pointing out those time-wasting actions which busy participants miss. The reminder's role is that of an observer, not critic or adviser.

In the pages that follow, these findings and suggestions are presented in some detail. We explain how we went about our observations and how we tried to correct the difficulties that were uncovered.

CHAPTER II

They Talk Past Each Other

"It takes," says Thoreau, in the noblest and most useful passage I remember to have read in any modern author, "two to speak truth—one to speak and another to hear." —Robert Louis Stevenson, "Truth of Intercourse," *Virginibus Puerisque*, J. M. Dent & Sons, 1925, p. 32.

How Misunderstanding Happens

The one thing people tend to take for granted when talking to others is that they understand each other. It is rare, indeed, in a meeting to have someone hold up his own argument long enough to say, "I think you said. . . . Did you?" or "Was I right in thinking you meant . . . ?" We found people ever so eager to parry what a man says without ever wondering whether *that* is what the man said.

In the give-and-take of talk things go fast, and one is so busy organizing his reply that he doesn't take the time to make sure he knows what he is replying to.

This is unfortunate because it often means that, instead of talking with others, people talk past or bypass each other.

Note some by-passings.

1. The British Staff prepared a paper which they wished to raise as a matter of urgency, and informed their American colleagues that they wished to "table it." To the American staff "tabling" a paper meant putting it away in a drawer and forgetting it. A long and even acrimonious argument ensued before both parties realised that they were agreed on the merits and wanted the same thing.[1]

2. I remember a worrisome young man who, one day, came back from the X-ray room wringing his hands and trembling with fear. "It is all up with me," he said. "The X-ray man said I have a hopeless cancer of the stomach." Knowing that the roentgenologist would never have said such a thing, I asked, "Just what did he say?" and the answer was on dismissing him, the roentgenologist said to an assistant, "N. P." In Mayo clinic cipher this meant "no plates," and indicated that the X-ray man was so satisfied with the normal appearance of the stomach on the X-ray screen that he did not see any use in making films. But to the patient, watching in an agony of fear for some portent of disaster, it meant "nothing possible:" in other words that the situation was hopeless![2]

3. A foreman told a machine operator he was passing: "Better clean up around here." It was ten minutes later

[1] Winston Churchill, "The Second World War," Vol. III, Book II, *The New York Times*, February 28, 1950, p. 31.

[2] Walter C. Alvarez, *Nervousness, Indigestion and Pain*, Paul B. Hoeber, Inc., 1943, p. 74.

when the foreman's assistant phoned: "Say, boss, isn't that bearing Sipert is working on due up in engineering pronto?"

"You bet your sweet life it is. Why?"

"He says you told him to drop it and sweep the place up. I thought I'd better make sure."

"Listen," the foreman flared into the phone, "get him right back on that job. It's got to be ready in twenty minutes."

. . . What [the foreman] had in mind was for Sipert to gather up the oily waste, which was a fire and accident hazard. This would not have taken more than a couple of minutes, and there would have been plenty of time to finish the bearing. Sipert, of course, should have been able to figure this out for himself—except that something in the foreman's tone of voice, or in his own mental state at the time, made him misunderstand the foreman's intent. He wasn't geared to what the foreman had said.[3]

4. Lady recently ordered some writing paper at a department store and asked to have her initials engraved thereon. The salesgirl suggested placing them in the upper right-hand corner or the upper left-hand corner, but the customer said no, put them in the center. Well, the stationery has arrived, every sheet marked with her initials equidistant from right and left and from top and bottom.[4]

5. In a private conversation with Mr. Molotov, it became apparent that another difficult misunderstanding in

[3] *The Foreman's Letter*, National Foreman's Institute, Inc., February 8, 1950, p. 3.

[4] "The Talk of the Town," *The New Yorker*, January 28, 1950, p. 21. Reprinted by permission. Copyright, 1950, The New Yorker Magazine, Inc.

language had arisen between ourselves and the Russians. At the San Francisco Conference when the question of establishing a trusteeship system within the United Nations was being considered, the Soviet delegation had asked Mr. Stettinius what the American attitude would be toward the assumption by the Soviet Union of a trusteeship. Mr. Stettinius replied in general terms, expressing the opinion that the Soviet Union was "eligible" to receive a territory for administration under trusteeship. Mr. Molotov took this to mean we would support a Soviet request for a trusteeship.[5]

In each case a word or phrase or sentence was used one way by the speaker and interpreted in another way by the listener. This is possible because words are versatile. Except for those intended for highly specialized purposes (like tetrasporangium, icosahedron, bisulfite), it is not unusual to find most words put to rather varied uses. A seventh-grade class in English was able to make up thirty sentences in which the word "set" was used differently each time. Even "word" is listed in sixteen different ways in *The American College Dictionary*.

The naïve speaker of a language usually has the feeling that, in general, words have a meaning, and he is seldom conscious of the great "area" of meaning for all except highly technical words. It is in this respect that the student's observation first needs widening and sharpening.

[5] James F. Byrnes, *Speaking Frankly*, Harper & Brothers, 1947, p. 96.

Frequently we have tried to "build vocabularies" by adding more units or words. But to push first the addition of more vocabulary units in order to increase the number of words may interfere with, rather than help, effective mastery of language. This is the process that produces a Mrs. Malaprop. Most frequently the student needs first to know well the various areas of use of the units he is already familiar with; he needs to be made conscious of the great diversity of uses or meanings for commonly used words. He must be made aware, for example, that the statement "The children did not *count*" can mean that they did not *utter the words* for the numbers in a series, or that the children *were not considered*. Ordinarily we just don't believe without considerable careful examination that for the five hundred most used words in English (according to the Thorndike *Word Book*) the Oxford Dictionary records and illustrates from our literature 14,070 separate meanings.[6]

At different times the same words may be used differently.

When Francis Bacon referred to various people in the course of his *Essays* as *indifferent, obnoxious,* and *officious,* he was describing them as "impartial," "submissive," and "ready to serve." When King James II observed that the new St. Paul's Cathedral was *amusing, awful,* and *artificial,* he implied that Sir Christopher Wren's recent creation was "pleasing, awe-inspiring, and skilfully achieved." When Dr. Johnson averred that Milton's *Lyci-*

[6] Charles C. Fries, "Using the Dictionary," *Inside the ACD,* October, 1948, p. 1.

das was "easy, vulgar, and therefore disgusting," he intended to say that it was "effortless, popular, and therefore not in good taste."[7]

The role of experience also affects the varieties of usage. Brander Matthews provided an example from a dinner-party conversation:

The second topic . . . was a definition of the image called up in our several minds by the word *forest*. Until that evening I had never thought of forest as clothing itself in different colors and taking on different forms in the eyes of different men; but I then discovered that even the most innocent word may don strange disguises. To Hardy forest suggested the sturdy oaks to be assaulted by the woodlanders of Wessex; and to Du Maurier it evoked the trim and tidy avenues of the national domain of France. To Black the word naturally brought to mind the low scrub of the so-called deer-forests of Scotland; and to Gosse it summoned up a view of the green-clad mountains that towered up from the Scandinavian fiords. To Howells it recalled the thick woods that in his youth fringed the rivers of Ohio; and to me there came back swiftly the memory of the wild growths bristling up unrestrained by man, in the Chippewa Reservation which I had crossed fourteen years before in my canoe trip from Lake Superior to the Mississippi. Simple as the word seemed, it was interpreted by each of us in accord with his previous personal experience.[8]

[7] Simeon Potter, *Our Language*, Pelican Books, 1950, p. 116.
[8] Brander Matthews, *These Many Years: Recollections of a New Yorker*, Charles Scribner's Sons, 1917, pp. 287–288. Quoted from

This conclusion about the range and possible uses of a word is easily verified. When it is forgotten, a listener just as easily comes to believe that (1) there is but one way to use a word—his—and (2) the speaker is doing with his words what the listener would were the listener doing the talking.

Can you see these beliefs at work in the examples given above?

In short, what you understand by any word or statement may not be what someone else intends to say. In a way, this is so obvious that most of us feel no obligation to think more about it. However, when one is aware of the fact it does not necessarily follow that he will act in terms of it. And there is some evidence that, unless people can be made sensitive to the possibility of by-passing, they make only meager efforts to stop it.

It Takes Two to Make Communication

I have no wish here to give comfort to the bore who gets so much pleasure squelching discussions with his defiant "Define your terms." His maneuver results in shifting the burden in communication to the other fellow. Both must be brought into the act. We would have the listener work just a bit, too. So we urge him to state his notion of what was being said. Inciden-

the essay by Allen Walker Read, "Linguistic Revision as a Requisite for the Increasing of Rigor in Scientific Method," read at the Third Congress on General Semantics, July 22, 1949.

tally, that bore may sometimes be routed with this: "What definition of my words have you in mind? Perhaps we are thinking together after all."

The "plain-talk" and "say-it-in-simple-words" teachers have been in vogue but they haven't been especially helpful. They, too, tend to put the emphasis on one side of the communication line. Putting the burden for understanding on the speaker is a kind of implied invitation to the listener to sit back and contentedly assume he has nothing to do but wait his turn. And besides, even the simple words have uses which too frequently vary between man and man.

We once observed eight meetings of a group of nine men, who functioned as a standing committee in a corporation having wide public responsibilities. Five had taken one or more courses and had studied some of the books on "talking plainly." One of the items checked had to do with "the assumption of understanding." Can men be differentiated according to their readiness to believe they know what the other fellow is referring to? We looked in their replies for such indications as *questions* for assurance that the asker is "with" the speaker, *qualifications* like "If I understand what you say" or "If I knew what you mean . . . ," *invitations* like "Correct me if I'm off the beam" or "Tell me whether I answered what you intended to say. . . ."

We were hardly prepared to find that four of the "plain-talk students" did the least amount of questioning, qualifying, inviting, etc. This may, of course, be an accident. Before a conclusion worth much can be drawn we should have a broader sampling of the population. And before a cause can be assigned with confidence much more investigation would be needed. Nevertheless, *these particular men*, knowing the ways to "plainness" and using them, tended to think they had done enough when they spoke so. They seemed to focus attention on *their* talking. They made no comparable effort to look to the character of what they heard.

I am not at all arguing that this finding in these particular cases means that training in plain talking makes for poor listening. I am trying to suggest only that training in the explicit effort at understanding may be a difficult sort of thing and may not automatically carry over from other training.

Cardinal Manning once said something relevant:

I have no doubt that I will hear that I am talking of what I do not understand; but in my defence I think I may say, I am about to talk of what I do not understand for this reason: I cannot get those who talk about it to tell me what they mean. I know what I mean by it, but I am not at all sure that I know what they mean by it; and those who use the same words in different senses are like men that run up and down the two sides of a hedge, and so can never meet.

It is helpful to think of the radio in this. The performer in the studio can talk his heart out, but if the man in the easy chair is tuned in elsewhere it really makes no difference what is being said. Unless the receiver is on the same wave length, the character of what is sent out hardly governs the communication process.[9]

This is not to imply that a speaker cannot help by putting what he has to say in clear, listenable language. Anything he does to define, simplify, amplify, illustrate, is all to the good. But it is only part of the process. The listener has a job to do, too. He must make the effort to come to terms with the speaker to keep from assuming that he inevitably knows what the speaker has in mind. At the very least he might temper his arrogance with a question now and then just to make sure.

It takes two to make communication.

Are You on His Communication Line?

The preceding pages of this chapter were mimeographed and given to three groups, one meeting for study of the Bible, one considering matters of policy in a business corporation, and one working on problems in the administration of a college fraternity. Every member of each group read a portion out loud. We then talked about the main point—it takes two to make communication. We agreed that this was rather

[9] This image is well developed in the article by Charles T. Estes, "Speech and Human Relations in Industry," *The Quarterly Journal of Speech*, April, 1946, pp. 160–169.

simple stuff and that we would try to talk with the possibility of by-passing in mind. We agreed, further, that no one of us would be insulted if asked to clarify or "talk some more" on any doubtful point. Nor would anyone feel hesitant about trying to get on the same wave length with anyone else. We gave each a small card with the inscription, "Are you on *his* communication line?"

What happened?

In each case the business of the meeting was slowed down. Only half as many items on the agenda could be covered. There was a certain amount of unfruitful wrangling about small points. Some members became tongue-tied in the face of so much freedom. Others became impatient with what seemed a waste of time, this trying to get to the speaker. The first sessions were always the worst. Most members felt comfortable only after the second or third.

And then we came upon something interesting. A man was being listened to. He found that others were actually waiting until he finished. He felt flattered in turn by the fact that another was trying to reach him rather than argue at him. He found himself trying to make his points so that his hearers would have less trouble with them. They were trying harder to read the cards he was putting on the table. The ornery member, normally so quick to doubt, stayed to question. The timid member found that the social pressure about the participation was all on his side.

We are inclined to think that the long-run results were worth the time and trouble.

The Purist's Dogma

In a number of experimental discussion groups generous enough to submit to such instruction there was a curious resistance to this seemingly obvious doctrine. I would be asked questions like these: Do you mean to say that a word doesn't have some definite, accurate meaning of its own regardless of the person who uses it? Isn't there a right or correct use for each word? If somebody fails to use a word exactly isn't he violating some rule in rhetoric or grammar?

How did these people come under the spell of the purist's dogma? Were they remembering some menacing drillmaster with a word list asking "What is *the* meaning of ———?" Or had they been badgered by vocabulary tests with entries like *glabrous heads: bald, over-sized, hairy, square, round; his stilted manner: irresolute, improper, cordial, stiffly formal* with instructions to circle the meaning? Or maybe they grew up when Alexander Woollcott was campaigning against certain current usage. He fought the use of "alibi" as a synonym for excuse; he wanted it saved for its "elsewhere" sense. He sneered when "flair" was used in the sense of knack or aptitude. He wanted it reserved for "capacity to detect." He and the traditional handbooks had a long list of such "reservations."

Or maybe they got their moorings from the pronouncements of Richard Grant White, who once said, "There is a misuse of words that can be justified by no authority, however great, and by no usage, however general." Or maybe they got no further in *Through the Looking Glass* than

". . . How old did you say you were?"

Alice made a short calculation, and said, "Seven years and six months."

"Wrong!" Humpty Dumpty exclaimed triumphantly. "You never said a word like it!"

"I thought you meant 'How old *are* you?' " Alice explained.

"If I'd meant that, I'd have said it," said Humpty Dumpty.

Regardless of the source, they used this dogma as the basis for a theory of their own about the cause of misunderstanding. If a speaker didn't use a word correctly it was only natural if a listener who did know the exact meaning was misled. Just get people to use words in their right meaning and then everyone will understand everyone else.

Indeed, this might be a way—but how can we do it? Who has the authority to declare *the* correct use and who has the time to learn it? There are more than 600,000 words in the Merriam-Webster unabridged dictionary and perhaps half as many more in the technical vocabularies of medicine, engineering, law, etc. And when the dictionary gives several meanings, which is *the* one? And just how is anyone going to curb those who, like Humpty Dumpty, would have their own ways with words:

". . . Impenetrability! That's what I say!"

"Would you tell me please," said Alice, "what that means?"

"Now you talk like a reasonable child," said Humpty Dumpty, looking very much pleased. "I meant by 'impenetrability' that we've had enough of that subject, and it would be just as well if you'd mention what you mean to do next, as I suppose you don't mean to stop here all the rest of your life."

"That's a great deal to make one word mean," Alice said in a thoughtful tone.

"When I make a word do a lot of work like that," said Humpty Dumpty, "I always pay it extra."

And what is more crucial, why do we look at words alone? Are words not most often used with other words in phrases, clauses, sentences? May not the setting affect the word?

We tried to get around this ill-advised zeal for exactness by suggesting that a word might be compared with a tool which can be used in a variety of ways. Thus, a screwdriver might be designed to drive screws, but once available it can be used to stir paint, jimmy a tight window, or, lacking any other weapon, to defend oneself with. You might, if you wish, insist that the screw function is the "right" or "correct" one and that a pistol is a much more effective weapon. But your insistence will hardly stop me from using the

screwdriver in these other ways if I find it convenient
or necessary to do so. A carpenter with a full rack of
tools may have good reason for reserving each for but
one use, but if some other purpose is served there is
nothing in the nature of the tool which could prevent
that other use. The desire for the restriction, then, is
personal rather than functional.

Within limits, especially in technical disciplines, it
is possible to standardize word usage. One is usually
safe in assuming that the workers in specialized areas
will conform to some established, stipulated word
usages. In the military establishment and in legal affairs, for example, it is often possible as well as necessary to insist that particular words be used in particular
ways.

Once outside the range of the specialist's interests,
however, we are wise if we expect words to be used
variously. A speaker's concern at any moment is not to
use a word but to make a statement. In his eagerness to
speak his piece he is more concerned with his continuous expression than with his total effect. If he
happens to range outside his listeners' conventional
usage, they will get nowhere lamenting his lexico-
graphical heresy. And if they do not get to his usage
they are likely to assume that he said what he never
intended to.

We have come to see wisdom in this advice: Never
mind what words mean. What did *he* mean?

It may take time to find out what a man means. It

may demand a patient listening and questioning. It may be an unexciting effort. But it should help to bring people into an area of awareness which they are too often on the outside of. Mr. Justice Jackson's experience in a situation more momentous than anything we were exposed to adds to our confidence in the advice:

It was my experience with the Soviet lawyers at Nurnberg that the most important factor in collaboration with the Soviet was patiently and persistently to make sure, when a proposition is first advanced, that it is thoroughly understood and that both sides are using their words to express the same sense. When this was done, the Soviet lawyers kept their agreements with us quite as scrupulously as American lawyers would. They may or may not regard that as a compliment, but my intentions are good. But it was my experience that it took infinite patience with them, as they thought it took infinite patience with us, to get to a point where there was a real meeting of minds as distinguished from some textual abstract formula which both could accept only because concretely it meant nothing or meant different things to each. And I have sometimes wondered how much misunderstanding could have been avoided if arrangements between the two countries had not often been concluded so hurriedly, in the stress of events, that this time-consuming and dreary process of reducing generalities to concrete agreements was omitted.[10]

[10] Excerpt from address by Mr. Justice Robert H. Jackson at the Bar Dinner of the New York County Lawyers' Association, December 8, 1949.

CHAPTER III

On a Certain Sort
of Disagreement

> To compel all men to employ the same collocation
> of words is impractical. The attempt has filled the
> world with controversy, and not brought us to the
> desired uniformity. I am so confident that nearly
> every general proposition is true, in the manner in-
> tended by the speaker, that I never contradict. —A. B.
> Johnson, *The Meaning of Words*, D. Appleton and
> Company, 1854, p. 182.

Would you like to make someone angry in discussion?

Call him a nasty name.

Tell him he sounds like a fugitive from an insane
asylum.

Interrupt him just as he is making his big point.

Anticipate his argument by a counterargument.

Insist he is biased because he has a special interest
in the case.

Or just contradict him.

In the course of post-discussion interviews with some 300 people, 70 percent of the participants said they felt few of the above activities more disturbing than a direct contradiction. As one woman put it, "When I say something and someone says, 'That's not so,' I feel just like screaming back, 'Yes, it certainly is so.'" A contradiction is an irritant, a kind of verbal jab in the face, an invitation to an angry answer. Even the thickest-skinned considered it distracting. The thin-skinned felt good only if they could retaliate.

Since so many people were bothered, we began to study this contradiction factor. After isolating several varieties, we concentrated on two and concluded that not much could be done by talking as such about this one:

when people were at odds on statements in which the items were indicated;

and that something had to be done about this one:

when people differed on statements in which the items referred to were not indicated.

Contradiction Involving Indicated Items

If I look at the clock and say that both hands point to 12 and if you look and say no, both hands point to 6, we have a clear-cut contradiction which can, perhaps, be resolved only by calling in other observers, an oculist, or a psychiatrist. There seems to be no way of preventing this sort of clash. Where it arises, the processes of majority decision usually govern.

Sometimes more looking helps. A group was shown a movie on soil conservation. In the discussion which followed, half the group insisted that the poorest land use was in the one-crop areas while the other half argued that the movie made no such conclusion possible. A rerun of the movie, along with an itemization (on which all agreed), revealed that neither group described the conditions accurately. Another time, a matron became rather violent in her denial of figures which permitted a man to say that the juvenile delinquency rate in her residential suburb was as great as in a poorer community nearby. She was shown the report prepared by the chief of police in her suburb. Even if the figures were hard to believe, at least the group was able to see what she was contradicting.

If there is no way to look again, or if after a second look the contradictory conclusions persist, maybe it would be best to take a vote—or just let the whole thing go.

Contradiction Involving Different Details

The specific item contradiction did not plague us as much as the one involving a difference in details. Just as a speaker may use a word in some restricted way, so he may make a statement which he intends to be applied to one particular set of details but which a hearer may take to apply to another set of details. So often when someone contradicts someone else, both are not talking about the same things. Man_1 has one set of details in mind while Man$_2$ focuses on a different set. Again and again in the analysis of conflict situations we found people talking against each other when they were, in fact, talking away from each other.

What they do then very much resembles the two men who collide on the street because each looks in a different direction. This physical bumping is understandable and unpreventable. But when people collide in talking because they fail to realize that each talker is intent on matters not considered by the other, it is unfortunate and preventable. The more we studied this variety of collision, the more we came to believe that *people ought to stop contradicting each other— unless they are perfectly clear as to the items involved.*

How It Happens

1. A man has one or more experiences with (or he may have read or heard about) a certain kind of person or situation.

2. Instead of making an Item Statement he moves more widely to a Catch-All Statement in which he may unknowingly intimate more details than he intends. It is one of the peculiarities of a Catch-All Statement that a man may use it (a) when he has a few details in mind, (b) when he has many, or (c) when he wants it to refer to all the items. Thus, an unwary or uncritical listener may tend to assume that the speaker is using the Catch-All Statement in its

broadest possibilities (i.e., c) when that might not be the case.

3. A listener hears the Catch-All Statement. He uncritically assumes the broadest use. He notes that in his experience the items he knows do not fit—that, indeed, his items differ in both substance and detail.

4. The listener then moves to his own Catch-All Statement, which contradicts the speaker's.

The controversy is, of course, without a basis unless the speaker intended that his Catch-All statement should apply to particulars he had no concern with. If the statement merely gives the impression of broader application, should not the listener make sure that that was the intention *before* he creates an issue? And before he goes on to miss what was being asserted?

What Happens

In the course of a discussion on taxation, the talk turned to the effects of great wealth on people.

Speaker$_1$: The wealthy are certainly happier than most of us. Take the young woman who inherited the dime-store fortune. Isn't she a lucky person?

Speaker$_2$: Why, no, she isn't lucky at all. I think she is probably one of the unhappiest persons in the U.S.

Before they began trading something more than verbal punches, each was asked to indicate the items covered by her statement.

Speaker$_1$ considered these details: (1) that the heiress did not have to worry about her income; (2) that if she wanted to buy something, the price was of little consequence.

Speaker₂ considered these details: (1) that the heiress had no settled home life; (2) that she couldn't walk downtown without a bodyguard.

These people were flagging trains on different tracks. Whatever the merit of the position taken by each it was at least a position which could only be dealt with in terms of the items which led to it. For one to contradict another without concern for these items is as relevant as the effort to judge the quality of fruit from the composition of the container.

X reports that Z hotel is excellent and its cooking first-class. On the strength of this Y goes to this hotel and is "very disappointed." His disappointment does not, however, lie in the hotel, but in his faith in abstractions. In the real world X was in room 29 and had a new spring mattress on his bed. But Y was in room 104 with an old mattress and where the horrid smell from the kitchen and the noise of an adjoining bathroom ruined his ease. Moreover, hotels do not cook—only humans do—and as the chef had meantime been sacked, and as his successor was a culinary pretender, the discomfiture of Y becomes understandable![1]

The man who said that "women can't be trusted" seemed to say "all" women or women "generally"—

[1] Thomas Robertson, *Human Ecology*, William Maclellan, 1948, p. 8.

but when he was quizzed he explained that his statement in fact referred to a series of specific situations in which certain females behaved deceitfully. The statement, in short, was about four cases.

Now, one might set out to contradict that man by a recital of four other cases in which certain trustworthy actions were demonstrated. But why act as if this denied the first assertion? If the man alludes to four particulars which lead to a Catch-All Statement, why is that statement scorned if it was not meant to apply to four other particulars? The man's statement applies to the cases it is used to refer to.

We are lost in controversy the moment a listener assumes that a speaker is referring to something different or something more than he could be found to refer to. If a listener chooses to conclude differently on the basis of a different set of cases, that certainly is his prerogative. But that difference must not be taken as the basis for a denial. Listeners must learn to "get to" the speakers. It is so easy to be content with the assumption that a Catch-All Statement necessarily means "all the cases." But that in turn means they misunderstand each other.

"I get no solace from religion," was the spark that set off a train of explosions one evening. "But, how absurd," another insisted. "Religion is the greatest source of solace in the world today." But the first man under questioning explained that the minister in his church was too newfangled, too eager to get people to engage in social-action projects, too interested in having people do things. "Too hectic for me," was the way he summarized the items to which the "no solace" statement applied. And to nothing else, we discovered. Behind the insister's statement, however, were phenomena quite outside the scope of our despondent man. They were at odds because the second man had chosen to contradict without considering what circumstances were involved in the first man's statement.

The troublesome contradiction factor comes into play, then, the moment someone neglects the items involved. Listeners are so busy paying attention to Catch-All Statements that they have no time for the items the speakers might be referring to. If the statement did not specify details, it was automatically taken to apply generally. But a statement, no matter how unlimited it may seem or how widely it may seem to apply, must be studied not for what it might allude to but for what it actually does or for what the speaker makes it allude to.

At an afternoon tea in New England, attended by members of both sexes, a woman made a remark to the effect that the English public school system tended to make men brutal. All in the group took sides, some agreeing and some disagreeing. A heated and lengthy discussion followed in which the merits and demerits of the English public school system were thoroughly reviewed. In other words, the statement was taken at its face value and discussed at that level. No one seemingly paid attention to the fact that the woman who made the statement had married an Englishman who had received an English public school education and that she was in the process of obtaining a divorce from him.[2]

The man who says "Labor leaders are racketeers" may be thinking of every labor leader, many labor leaders, 40 percent of the labor leaders, some labor leaders—or his statement may come from his reading in the morning paper of the imprisonment of two union men on a charge of embezzlement. Should not an adequate counterstatement take account of the cases the man had taken account of?

It is just possible that the maker of a Catch-All Statement believes it to have some universal application. But if he does, he ought not be disturbed if someone else finds items to which it does not apply. If he insists on the universal application, then the disagreement can be centered on the scope of the particulars and the conflict pinned to them rather than to the statement whose coverage was only to be inferred.

A man, after reading about premarital sexual relations among students in a high school in a midwestern city, asserts that "Parents no longer care about what happens to their children. If they did, they'd see to it that things like that didn't happen." He was immediately set upon by a half-dozen parents who proceeded to assert that "Present-day parents are no worse than

[2] F. J. Roethlisberger and W. J. Dickson, *Management and the Worker*, Harvard University Press, 1939, pp. 273–274.

their parents." On questioning, the man said that though his statement was prompted by the story he had read, it might apply all over.

We now have a choice. If he meant that there was a situation in one high school related to one set of parents, then someone might counter with what he knew of the situation in another high school, and the argument would be grounded on the difference. But if he meant that this did apply further and more widely, then the resolution of the matter would depend on investigation of more situations. In either case, the controversy without the clarification would surely have moved in the mists of verbalism far from the intentions of the participants.

What to Do

Our object is not the elimination of Catch-All or Broad Conclusion Statements.

We would try only to help people in discussion find the ground on which they contradict one another—whether on the items or on the statement.

Give us the items, the instances, the data to which you allude. Then, no matter how sweeping your statement or how grand your generalization, we will know what we must consider. If we look only to what your language implies, we may go beyond your intention. To keep within the framework of your meaning we must stay with your particulars. We may even have to ask you for them.

Justice Holmes once held, "I always say the chief

end of men is to form general propositions—adding that no general proposition is worth a damn."

The position we take here is somewhat different. It does not even say that speakers should hesitate about making general statements. It does say that when they do, listeners have no adequate ground for agreement or dissent. That can come when the items are brought out into the open. Nor is anyone justified in saying that another's Catch-All Statement is meaningless. Before coöperation with and clarification by the speaker a listener doesn't know what it means. Indeed, the statement may be so broadly meaningful that a listener may think something else is being referred to than what is.

The "philosophers" who make their grand generalizations can, in effect, be saying so much or so little that one had better hesitate before saying yes or no. It is much better to wait for the "for instances." For if they are the substance of his position, what looked like a matter for nay-saying may be something on which agreement is possible. If our "philosopher" is unwilling to indicate the particulars to which he refers, we had better forgo our 'tis-'tain'ts. If we have no way of getting on *his* line why do we presume to act as if we are on it?

Too Easy Agreement

The members of an Adult Study Group, which tried to take this habit-of-looking-to-the-items seriously, discovered for themselves the fact that occasionally when no one is moved to question a Catch-All Statement it might be wise in the interests of intelligent understanding to do it deliberately. They learned that too quick agreement on the Catch-All Statement might be a mixed blessing if it concealed a disagreement which was sure to show up if the people stopped to ask about the items involved.

The discovery came about in this way. During "Brotherhood Week" in 1949 they had had a fine go on the necessity of building better human relations among all people. The twenty-one attending had heard a panel describe the unfortunate effects of prejudice and discrimination, ending in a plea for attitudes of neighborliness and good will.

Two weeks later one of the members interested in the establishment of a state-wide Fair Employment Practices Commission, designed to prevent discriminatory employment practices, tried to get signatures for a petition to the legislature. She found twelve of the participants in the discussion unwilling to sign. What aroused her was the fact that ten of the people prefaced their objections by statements like "Of course, I am in favor of eliminating discrimination but . . ." followed by a listing of reasons and details suggesting that the legislation was undesirable.

At the insistence of this member, the group met to spend an evening to talk about this phenomenon. There were few dull moments. Charges of hypocrisy, lip service to ideals, and un-Christian behavior were sandwiched between assertions of bureaucratic practices, the desirability of moving slowly, the need for more education, "You can't legislate people into goodness," etc. The note of aggressiveness by the nine willing to sign was matched by the defensiveness of the unwilling twelve. Just about the time the group tension was well marked the leader, with some hesitation, asked whether they might try to put the theory-about-the-statements to work. Is it not possible, he wondered, that people who saw eye to eye on the Catch-All Statement might honestly see quite differently on the Item Statements? Could people have notions about the one without appearing hypocritical when they had differing notions on the other? Both factions (when their excitement had eased) were able to take comfort from this formulation. It was, they saw, all too easy to assume that an agreement on the Catch-All meant agreement on the Items, that the trouble lay not in the honesty or dishonesty of the participants but in their acceptance of a statement which implied what was by no means inevitable.

The problem now is to move from feelings of disappointment about the "inconsistency of attitudes" or the "gap between belief and action" to an analysis of the Items. Maybe, when *they* are squarely faced, a new and deeper resolution of the difficulty can be obtained.

What to Do When the Contradiction Creates a Gulf

I must make an admission.

A number of radio forums and panel discussions are

interesting because (among other things) there is so much conflict. In a way the package of several speakers, a big subject, and little time encourages a clash of views because the speakers have to cover so much ground in their few minutes that they are moved to lash out indiscriminately at each other without having the time to discover whether they differ on the Big Statements or on the Items. Lest sponsors of these programs quarrel with me because I seem to imply this of all the programs I hasten to note that I have in mind at least twenty broadcasts of four different programs. I am not decrying the use of the discussion situation for its dramatic values. It may well be that the very sharpness of the give-and-take holds the attention of an audience who might turn off a program in which the participants sought deliberately to get an understanding of each other.

I readily admit that tackling the contradiction factor may be a dull business. I would, however, plead this: that our goal is a group facing of problems in an atmosphere of understanding rather than in one which neglects the understanding because of the need for dramatic effects.

What, in short, may be good for radio may not be so good around the bargaining table, in the committee room, or in the judge's chamber.

In these circumstances we used a little formula whenever a contradiction led to a heated rejoinder. The leader (or anyone else) would (1) ask the speakers to remake their statements; (2) ask each to give the items he was alluding to; (3) ask the other whether he was objecting to the Items or the impression that the Catch-All Statement alluded to some other or all the possible items.

Whenever there was a chance to prepare a group ahead of time against the disruptive effects of the contradiction factor, we found it useful to explain that many a friction point might be smoothed down faster (or might never develop) if each was able to locate the *point of trouble.*

It was helpful if it was realized that a statement could be about a number of possibilities.

1. One might refer explicitly to specific, itemized cases, particulars, or details.

2. One might talk in statements which seem to refer indefinitely, generally, in unlimited fashion to many cases, particulars, or details, when in fact the speaker is alluding to one or more specific ones. Here the items are not explicitly indicated in the statement, though they are in the speaker's awareness.

3. One might talk in statements which may seem to refer indefinitely, generally, in unlimited fashion to many items when in fact the speaker had reference to no clearly indicated ones or when his statements seem to be applying to some, many, or all the items involved. Here the items are neither explicitly indicated in the statement nor clearly defined in the speaker's mind.

In brief, then, a contradiction of an Item Statement might ultimately be resolved by further looking. Contradictions based on non-specifying statements are often dissolved when the items over which there is a difference are exposed. When the speaker could give no items it was rarely wise to take issue with him, because there was little on which such arguing could be based. Far better was it to stop and help him locate some.

In his *Discourse on Method* Descartes made a similar point: "The diversity in our opinions does not proceed from some men being more rational than others, but solely from the fact that our thoughts pass through diverse channels and the same objects are not considered by all."

CHAPTER IV

Jon Stone and the Fools Across the Table

It is the mark of real self-assurance, the sign of inner strength, to be conciliatory and respectful and understanding of the neighbor's point of view. There is no uglier tendency in American nature than the quickness to moral indignation and to wild suspicions of bad faith which many of us display when other people do not think as we do. —From a speech, "The National Interest of the United States," by George F. Kennan at Northwestern University, January, 1951.

There is another great source of misunderstanding: not that men see different details, but that they see the same details differently. In this, there is no mistaking of word use or confusion of items, but a more fundamental divergence which seems rooted in the very patterns of perceiving.

What one man likes, another dislikes. What disturbs one leaves another cold. What frightens him encourages her. What this man would discard, that man would save. What moves one to pity stirs the other to anger.

Something happens in a discussion when people thus disagree. The talk is spirited. There are more interruptions. More people want to say more. Dull moments are few. The battle front moves between the issues and the men. Speakers get assertive; their voices sharpen; they listen for the moment in the flow of talk when they may break in.

As the talk situation becomes more dramatic the conflict deepens. If the people see eye to eye it is only because they are glaring at each other.

What do you do then? The chairman may cry "peace" and he may get it—by adjourning the meeting. Once such disagreement is out it is not easy to stop it. You may stop the talk but not the human differing. That can, perhaps, only be understood.

Patterns of Disagreement

We set out to catalogue the expressions of dissent. Do disagree-ers face up to each other in the same way? Five patterns appeared most often.

1. *The inquiring-investigative attitude*, in which one states his position and shows that he is willing to listen some more. "No, I don't believe that, but will you explain why you do? . . . That's not how I see it; tell me why you don't see it my way. . . . I don't like it at all; now why do you favor it? . . ."

2. *The air of incredulity*, in which the speaker does not invite further explanation but in which he doesn't refuse it either. He is usually decent enough to let the other fellow contribute even though he'd prefer not to. He listens, though somewhat grudgingly. "I can't for the life of me understand why you think that. . . . When all our experience points the other way, it is certainly strange to see you disagree. . . . How did you ever get that idea? . . . Every now and then a man has to put up with an idea like that, but really now. . . ."

3. *The inclination to laughter*, in which one lets everybody know in a good-natured manner that what the other fellow proposes just doesn't deserve mature consideration. He creates the impression that even if he listens it won't do any good. He isn't impatient, just amused. He is gently derisive, not angry. "Now, I ask you, gentlemen, isn't that the silliest (funniest, craziest, most childish) thing you ever heard? . . . Well, that's what you get when you let a man have a hearing. . . . Let's not be too rough on Bill, he's been working too hard. . . ."

4. *The expression of suspicion and distrust*, in which we hear a note of resentment. The speaker comes out and (sometimes politely) accuses another of trying to take unfair advantage. He would really like to get away from the proposal but he is content to tell off the accused man. The feeling of bad faith asserted and understood is usually followed by a counter-imputation and a categorical denial. "That's just so you people will get all the benefits. . . . Where's the payoff? What's in it for you? . . . All this is covering up something. Why

aren't you honest with us? . . . That's a typical _____ (insert any stigma word) way of doing things. . . ."

5. *The mood of dismissal,* in which a man makes it clear that he wishes to go no farther, to talk no more about something which is to him impossible, unthinkable, wrong, unnecessary, or just plain out of the question. He has spoken and there is little use in trying to make him see otherwise. If he has his way there will be no more discussion on the matter. "It won't work and that's all there is to it. . . . I refuse to listen to any more of this nonsense. . . . Anybody who comes to such a conclusion has something wrong with him. . . . We've never worked that way before and we aren't going to start now. . . ."

There are other patterns of disagreement but we learned to spot evidence of these rather quickly. However, it wasn't until we met Jon Stone that what we were studying came into focus for us. He became the prototype of a very particular problem. (Jon Stone is no one person. He is a composite of many, a kind of vessel into which many details of a certain kind of intransigence were poured. I have, however, listened to some men and women who bore a disturbing resemblance to the character described here.)

Jon Stone was the treasurer of a company doing several million dollars' worth of business annually. He was, according to his associates, a good man—until he got into a conference. Then there was trouble; he was impatient with anything outside the range of his preferences. So long as the issue was a friendly one he was helpful, shrewd. But when something was presented that he had reason to dislike, he became an inconsiderate, impatient, and caustic critic. He was never afraid of suggesting that those who analyzed things differently didn't know what they were talking about. He didn't imply that they were dishonest. They just showed poor judgment. They just didn't know. He rarely quit arguing when outvoted. He simply used the vote as an indication that a majority could be wrong, too. It was hard to talk with Jon around. Many had the feeling that when they stopped Jon would pounce.

Jon Stone was a kind of gentleman bully. His creed seemed to consist of this: If you believed something and if you kept insisting that you were right, sooner or later you would wear the others down and they might came around to your way of seeing things.

Jon was comfortable in his tight little world. He liked what he knew. He had fixed perspectives which were "right" to him. Any other way of looking at things was wrong. Jon was not ignorant. He knew much. He had been trained well, in school and on the job. But his training had incapacitated him for just one thing: the recognition that people could see details differently. "Facts are facts, aren't they?" "Both of us can't be right" were his clinchers.

What Jon Stone helped us to understand was this:

that we ought to look not only at the disagreement but also at the mood in which it was expressed. When someone disagreed in the inquiring mood, the other fellow was often encouraged to make efforts in accommodation. But let the note of suspiciousness or dismissal sound and overt hostility was its echo.

Jon Stone seemed unable to disagree without getting disagreeable. The longer we listened to him, the more we analyzed his statements, the clearer it seemed that he did not understand how another could in all reason come to conclusions different from his. He helped us to see that a disagreement could be creative or disruptive depending for the most part on the assumption which a disagree-er made about the character and capacity of those with whom he differed. When the disagree-er assumed that another was a fool to believe as he did the talk became a continuous growl. It was to characterize his way of thinking that La Rochefoucauld must have written: "We find scarcely any person of good sense save those who agree with us." It was clear that Jon Stone never had George Washington's insight: "And shall I arrogantly pronounce that whosoever differs from me, must discern the subject through a distorting medium or be influenced by some nefarious design? The mind is so formed in different persons as to contemplate the same object in different points of view. Hence originates the difference on questions of the greatest import, both human and divine."

This communication breakdown, in short, comes not from a misunderstanding of what was said but from a failure to understand how another could with good reason say that.

Can anything be done about it?

In the first place, the objectives must be clear. Do we want Jon Stone to agree with everything he hears? Do we want him willy-nilly to give up the views which grew out of his experience? Not at all. We want Jon Stone to do little more than reconsider his assumption that the people across the table are stupid just because they see things differently. This is not to say that anything goes, that any proposal, prediction, or conclusion is as good as any other. It is to suggest only that utterances which imply that if-he-has-ideas-at-variance-with-mine-then-he-is-a-fool do not lead to fruitful discussion between men. The automatic classification of those who do not agree with us as incompetent or stupid is a spark that sets off too many dialectical explosions.

This goal is, of course, a modest one. It falls far short of that deeper kind of rapport Dr. Harry Stack Sullivan described in his *Conceptions of Modern Psychiatry*: "In dealing with students, with patients, or with any group or nation the first step is to see the world through their eyes, to enter into what they are trying to do, however strange their behavior seems. Genuine communication is impossible on any other basis."

But let not the very modesty of our goal becloud its importance.

Let me restate the goal. *It is to help the members of a group preserve some respect for each other. It is to make explicit the awareness that differences in judgment need not mean that those on one side are wise and those on the other foolish. It is to try to get each man to look at the image he has created of those around him.*

In the course of our studies we saw a number of individuals try to deal with the Jon Stones. Sometimes they quit in dismay, with a feeling of hopelessness. Some told us afterwards that nothing could be done so long as he was around. Sometimes they tried the soft answer as a way of dissolving the wrath. But more than once the Jon Stones took this as a sign of weakness. Sometimes they replied in kind, returning charge with countercharge. But this usually led to more of the same.

This experience led us to believe that if some of the unpleasant effects of men disagreeing disagreeably were to be eliminated we would need some scheme by which to take the burden away from individuals. We needed a way by which a group could deal with the disagreement situation, a problem as important as the issue itself. In short, if a group was faced with the disintegration that accompanies disagreement it had two problems rather than one to deal with.

By good fortune we were able to test this belief in

Jon Stone's office. He was a member of an executive committee deadlocked on the matter of the company's employee-promotion policies. The president of the company was distressed at the depth and character of the disagreement. Some refused to believe that changes in existing policy would be desirable; some wanted sharper definitions of the seniority provisions; others argued for more elaborate merit ratings. Jon Stone's recalcitrance had been matched around the room during each of several meetings.

Because it was apparent that such wrangling could have few useful outcomes, it was possible to persuade the president that a meeting or two might well be given over to talk about the group's purposes instead of the promotion issue. These questions should be considered: What do differences in judgment mean? What should be done about differences in judgment?

It was decided to approach the discussions through a memorandum on the origin and inevitability of differences in point of view. Consideration of this document was to be the only item of business the next meeting. The president sent it to each member of the committee along with a note asking each man to analyze and present comments on one of the items. The memorandum is produced herewith.

Why Men Disagree. Observers have written widely about the character of human disagreement. Here is a sampling:

1. When Enid tells Dr. Talley (in S. N. Behrman's

The Talley Method, Random House, 1941, p. 194) that she will not marry him, he says, "My God, you're not going to let a difference in point of view separate us!" She replies, "But that's all that ever does separate people."

2. When two fellows bump into each other on the street, it is either because they are not looking at all, or because they are looking at something else. Most of us have done that at one time or another. Differences of opinion are somewhat similar, in that they result, not from a collision because two chaps are both watching a pretty girl, but because each is seeing a different picture of events as they are and may become.

One man looks ahead to the right of the road and sees a shining green plain, with waving grass and browsing cattle. His companion looks ahead to the left of the road and sees it curving around a long smooth hill, with jagged peaks and cliffs showing in the distance. "Hold on," he cautions. "There are cliffs and rocks. We had better camp and wait for morning."

Each is telling the truth, each is seeing clearly—and each is looking at something entirely different. There is not much to choose between the logical reasoning of one man and that of another, nor between their general objectives. Sometimes they are looking in different directions, and sometimes they are wearing colored glasses that emphasize different sets of facts. —Royal F. Munger's column "Old Bill Suggests" in *The Chicago Daily News*, April 30, 1941.

3. Everyone knows that two persons belonging to different cultures may react in diametrically opposite ways if

there are different established norms relating to the situation at hand. Present freshly broiled pork chops to hungry men. One of our hungry men is a Mohammedan whose religion tells him that anything connected with pigs is disgusting—this is an established taboo, a norm. The other person is a Christian. He will seize the chops and eat them with gusto. The first person will not only not touch the chops, he will be filled with disgust both for them and for the person who eats such filthy things. This is one example, on a highly complicated level, of a very simple psychological fact, that there is no point-to-point correlation between external stimulation and the experience aroused by it, or the subsequent behavior. . . .

There is no point-to-point correlation between a physical stimulus and the experience and subsequent behavior it arouses; the experience and the behavior may be, to a large extent, a function of the state of the organism at the time. Take a cardboard of uniform orange color about two feet long and one foot wide. Cover half of the cardboard with a black paper and look at the uncovered orange part steadily for some minutes, and then remove the black cover. For some time the covered part will appear a different shade of orange from the other part. The same gray may look darker or brighter according to the white or black surroundings, or the general pattern in which, or beside which, it is found. The same tone may arouse different effects when alone and when preceded or followed by other tones in a melody. Similarly, within limits, a sound is judged high or low, a weight heavy or light, not only in accordance with its absolute physical value, but also in accordance with the background of sounds or weights that precede. —Muzafer Sherif in *The Psychology of Social Norms,* Harper & Brothers, 1936, pp. 28–29.

4. Some years ago I happened to be present at a Manlaslo, a gypsy tribal tribunal. They were judging a man for polygamy.

"But why?" I asked. "Your tribe is polygamous."

"Yes," the chief answered. "But his tribe isn't. He broke the laws of his tribe. We are judging him according to the rules of his tribe." —Konrad Bercovici in "The Wisdom of the Illiterate," *Golden Book Magazine,* May, 1934, p. 559.

5. When a psychiatrist is treating a patient, it sometimes happens that the patient is extremely insulting. In such circumstances the psychiatrist will restrain his natural impulse to punch the patient on the nose and will try to find out why the patient feels that way. The reason for this reaction is that the accumulated experience of the profession shows that when you punch patients on the nose you do little to advance the treatment. If such punches helped patients, they would be commonly practiced, since they would be much milder than some forms of treatment patients now undergo, for instance, electric shock. The experience is, however, that retaliation puts a stop to further treatment. There is cancellation of the physician's opportunity to help the patient improve his relations with people. On the other hand, when the physician learns why the patient has such an unfavorable impression and traces out some of the causes, he often finds he has arrived at the center of some of the patient's deepest conflicts and difficulties. Inquiry gives an opportunity for therapy and ad-

justment which involves successful changing of the patient's images and attitudes. . . .

False images of ourselves as a nation produce barriers to understanding our position in relation to other nations and the consequences, particularly the indirect consequences, of our acts. Thus, we may think we are being co-operative when actually we appear weak. Or, on the other hand, what seems to us a demonstration of reasonable firmness may strike another country as an overt act of hostility requiring immediate retaliation. What we suppose is a generous effort to give support may be angrily treated as an attempt at exploitation. We are confident that we will never, without provocation, attack any nation with atomic bombs and so we discount the threat element in our possession of the weapon, while other nations with a different view of us never forget it.

When difficulties arise, we have a tendency to write off the behavior of another country as unreasonable, as due to peculiarities of its innate nature, or as the product of evil leaders with evil intentions. Other countries in their turn do the same regarding our behavior. Such conclusions may, at times, be just in terms of certain premises, but the trouble with them is that, just or not, they are a dead end. They do not lead to solving the problem. They lead to giving up, or to one of the well-established patterns of hitting back. There is no blindness like the blindness of self-righteousness. Inquiry and cool thinking with adequate perspective habitually cease to function at the time they are most necessary. In their place comes back talk, heightened emotions, hair-trigger readiness, misinterpretations and the taking of positions from which pride makes retreat impossible.—Taken from *Human Relations in a Changing World*, by Alexander H. Leighton, copyright, 1949, Alexander H. Leighton, published by E. P. Dutton & Co., Inc., New York, pp. 104–106.

6. Different minds will take the same events in very different ways. A tribe of Congo negroes will react quite differently to (say) its first introduction to the story of Christ's passion, than did the equally untutored descendants of Norsemen, or the American Indians. Every society meets a new idea with its own concepts, its own tacit, fundamental way of seeing things; that is to say, *with its own questions*, its peculiar curiosity. —Suzanne Langer, *Philosophy in a New Key*, Harvard University Press, 1942, p. 6.

What could be expected? Would the staff discuss the memorandum as some foolish notion? Would they see its relevance? Would they say, "Of course we know this. Now let's go about our business?" Would they take offense at this implied criticism of their difficulties?

The president opened the meeting with some carefully planned words about his interest in the company and his desire for the improvement of its operation. He was impressed, he continued, with the loyalty of the company officers and their interest in the company's welfare. He was distressed, however, with their difficulties in arriving harmoniously at solutions to their problems. He wondered whether it would be worth while to give some time to the reasons why people differed so. He hoped they would understand that this departure from their business was a temporary one. And might there be a discussion of each of the items in the memorandum. Might it begin with Bill. "Do you think S. N. Behrman was saying anything that is true and meaningful for us?" They spent an hour and ten minutes at that session and an hour and twenty-five minutes the next time before they had commented on all the items. At the next meeting they returned to the promotion problem.

What follows is a condensation of a stenographic report of the president's answer to this question raised two months later: What good did it do?

This thing is baffling. I can't put my finger on it. They were a little slow in opening up. I think they resisted because they weren't sure what I was up to but I kept at them. When Jon Stone said there were other things besides "a difference in point of view" that separated people they became interested in trying to pin him down. They had a good time trying to say that Munger's explanation was too simple. But they didn't show how. So far as I can see only one definite thing happened. They saw what we were driving at, that a different point of view on things was possible. When we met on the promotion-policy afterwards we didn't lick it. We're still at it. It is a very knotty problem, but, you know, there has been less of that meanness we had been having. We may not solve the promotion program to everybody's satisfaction but whatever we do there isn't going to be so much bloodshed. Maybe the talk about the doctor's punching the patient not helping the treatment was a good thing because it gave our men a new slant. Maybe they became afraid to hit out at those who wouldn't agree with them, afraid someone would remind them of the doctor and the patient. I don't believe many of the men will be readily converted to each other's ideas, but I do think we're going to be able to discuss the problems without so much thinking the other fellow doesn't know what he's talking about. What will interest you is the fact that Harlow [one of the men who had said that nothing could be done so long as "he" was around] stood up to Jon Stone at one point and almost made him listen. I'm thinking now of asking you to do another memo for us on some more aspects of the disagreement matter which we can talk about 3 or 4 months from now.

The memorandum approach has been used with three other staffs. In general the effects have been about the same. These impressions have emerged from the reports of the chairmen:

1. This will not work unless the chairman is thoroughly coöperative and willing to take the time (at least two sessions) to make the reconditioning process operative.

2. There is no special excellence in the memorandum reproduced here. Any one which contains the germinal notions should work. This particular one had only the virtue of novelty.

3. The use of this tactic does not insure a solution for a tough problem.

4. This approach is valuable because it is so direct.

It provides some common ground for a group. When someone says something violent against another's view each man has the force of a common opinion justifying and supporting him should he choose to reply differently. Without that common opinion he is just one man making an argument. To say this another way: the disagreement theory evolved from discussion of the memorandum served as a judgment on higher ground to which anyone could appeal. Jon Stone no longer stood on the privileged ground. The objects of his wrath were now there.

5. The approach seemed to give individuals in a group a feeling of confidence that even though they were at odds it was possible to work things out because the disagreement was not necessarily based on the others' stupidity or irrationality.

CHAPTER V

Getting Problem-Centered

> The universe is not to be narrowed down to the
> limits of the understanding, which has been men's
> practice up to now, but the understanding must be
> stretched and enlarged to take in the image of the
> universe as it is discovered.—Francis Bacon, *Parasceve*,
> Aphorism 4.

Alexander Meiklejohn once said, "So far as minds
are concerned, the art of democracy is the art of thinking independently together."

Around the cracker barrel, in the club car, or at a
cocktail party it is important that men keep on talking.
The more independent the thinking is, the greater is
the incentive to more talk. In a staff, board, or committee meeting where work has to be done, that, plus
something more, is needed—a feeling of togetherness,
a sense of common effort. Some groups have it, some
lose it, some never get it. Why?

What follows is not an answer. It is rather (1) a theory and (2) an approach with which to deal with a tiny bit of the question.

The theory says that the sense of togetherness is diminished whenever people get "solution-minded" too quickly.

The approach requires a leader to do everything he can to keep people "situation-minded."

If what we saw in discussions is typical of what goes on elsewhere, then this can be said: People are ever so eager to *prescribe* for problems and loath to *describe* them. Let someone hint at a difficulty or existing evil, and ready-made panaceas are offered around the room. Regardless of their position, education, or experience, these people were well stocked with answers. In the week before this paragraph was written I sat in on a meeting in which forty of the first forty-seven minutes were taken up with proposals guaranteed to correct troubles which were not analyzed until the following twenty minutes. About thirty of the forty-seven minutes had been wasted on proposals quite unrelated to the needs as revealed.

I once asked a staff to make one-word comments about

- A surgeon who ordered an operation when the patient complained of a pain in the stomach before the source of the pain was located;
- A judge who handed down his decision after the reading of the indictment;

- A general who devised an invasion scheme without review of the intelligence reports;
- A hunter who shot before sighting his quarry.

The words mentioned most frequently were: reckless, stupid, unwise. Yet this same group considering a proposal for internal reorganization had given only five of the first fifty-one minutes of their talk to pinpointing the areas in which a change was needed. Teachers will bear witness that one of the reasons students do poorly on exams is their eagerness to write an answer even before they understand the question. If the answers are "interesting but irrelevant" it is hardly surprising.

There was, in the groups we studied, a deeply held assumption that because the problem was announced it was understood. People seemed too often to consider a complaint equivalent to a description, a charge the same as the specification.

Does this make any difference?

Whenever a group dodged the labor of description to move straight for solutions we noted these unhappy side effects:

1. The tendency to partisanship was encouraged. Participants set right out to defend their pet proposals. "Here is the answer" was the theme of those who were sure they had private pipe lines to the sources of salvation. Then the discussion went off in a doctrinal mist on the cogency of the answers *unrealistically disregarding the difficulties to be corrected.*

2. This cart-before-the-horse procedure, by keeping the group from seeing exactly what needed correction, was almost always time-wasting. Before long someone would point out that an aspect of the situation was being neglected. Some of the group would then want to look back to see if this was so. The men-with-the-answers were rarely willing to admit any deficiencies in their proposals. The ensuing wrangle was fun for the observers, but it seemed not to lead to creative coöperation.

By failing to survey the situation a group had little chance to get the feeling of togetherness that accompanies a common exploration. Some of the happiest examples of group rapport we saw were those in which members began the talk by a ruthless ruling out of everything which did not add to their picture of the situation. Not what-should-we-do-about-it? but what-is-it-that-has-gone-wrong? is the question that keeps a group from the centrifugal tendencies of the solution-minded.

If there is specific truth in the adage that "men support what they help to create," then an excess of zeal for answers is one way to keep a group from the feeling of common effort that goes with a sense of the situation to be corrected.

The Map of the Situation

What to do? We work for the achievement of problem-mindedness through the leader.

The leader is urged (in a training session away from the group) to visualize at the outset a large uncharted map to be filled in by what those in the group know, by what they have found or observed themselves, by what they have read or heard from others. He does everything possible to urge them to tell all they know about the conditions, circumstances, factors, details, happenings, relationships, changes, disturbances, effects. What have you observed? What have others observed? These are the questions he keeps asking of them. When they have replied, the group will have a map of the situation, a picture in varying degrees of fullness.

There will be holes and blank spots and some of the fillings-in will be faint and uncertain. Some places on the map will be doubtful because asserted by some and denied by other members. Some of the observations may have been fleeting or superficial or marginal because the observers were interested in something else at the time. Nevertheless, if our leader keeps to his prodding role he will have helped the group sight the quarry—as a common effort. When he has been most effective, members of the group may be moved to realize that the filled-in map is the product of *their* collective knowledge. I have been told repeatedly by observers that people in a group seem to have a heightened regard for each other when they have jointly contributed what they know before they get into the turmoil of partisanship that seems so much a part of deciding what to do.

On occasions we've seen a miracle—people admitting (without rancor but with disappointment) that they did not know enough about a problem to deal with it sensibly. When this has led to a discussion about what must be done to get more information, the spirit of joint endeavor is really something to see. I have never seen this spirit in a group which sought solutions first.

Training the Leader

In addition to coaching the leader in his role as "prodder" we have found some values (whenever it was possible to get him for a couple of hours more) in a program designed to deepen the leader's own problem-mindedness. This program was in two parts. One sought to help him recognize the kinds of statements people made which might or might not be problem-centered. The second tried to emphasize the fact that "every" human problem required a focus on the situation.

Here is a sketch of the instructional scheme.

Let's say that in your city there is a slum area of eleven square blocks and that people are beginning to suspect that the housing conditions may be involved in an increase in ill health and delinquency in that area.

Let's suppose that you are moved to talk *about* the situation. You could make these basic statements.

1. *Statements which refer to what was observed:* That such and such kinds of illness and delinquency were found

by you or someone else, that the number was greater than or different from that in other years, that they were in such and such ratio to those in other areas, that they were to be observed in this or that circumstance, that these individuals were involved in this or that way, etc.

These statements presuppose that someone was observing from some point of view and that if others had been in his position they would make rather similar statements. There will, of course, be a margin of error since others cannot be in exactly his position.

2. *Statements which refer to what is assumed:* Since it is hardly possible for any group of people to be everywhere at once or to have access to all that goes on or to be able to account for everything that happens or to be able to foresee all that will happen, there must be places on the map they will have to fill in with their guesses, inferences, suppositions, assumptions. They will then make statements about what they believe to be the case.

We should expect the widest possible discrepancy in this phase of the talk. There are no fences around the imaginative capacities. A man can guess freely and readily. If there is reason to look for essential agreement on what can be observed (from any given point of view) it is rather understandable if the widest disagreement arises when men are stating their assumptions about what was not observed. A long step in the direction of clarity will, however, be taken when participants see the difference between statements of observation and assumption.

This is not the same as the distinctions between right and wrong facts and conclusions.

Lincoln won a big reputation as a corporation counsel. He defended a big railroad in one case that involved hundreds of thousands of dollars. The prosecuting attorney's summation was a masterpiece of logic and eloquence, and took three hours to deliver. Mr. Lincoln amazed the court by limiting his rebuttal to a single sentence: "My opponent's facts are right, but his conclusion is wrong." The jury burst into laughter, retired, and promptly brought in a verdict in Lincoln's favor.

That evening the two attorneys dined together, and Lincoln's disgruntled adversary said, "I'd give a lot to know how you hornswoggled that jury with one short sentence."

"I'll tell you about that," drawled Lincoln. "Last night I had the privilege of downing a few drinks at the tavern with the judge and the gentlemen of the jury, and in the course of the evening I told them the story of the farmer's little boy who came running into the house one night to report, 'Say, Father, the hired hand is out in the barn with the new serving maid, and they're keeping the hay warm.' The farmer answered, 'Son, your facts are right but your conclusion is wrong.' I wouldn't be surprised if the jury remembered that story in the courtroom this morning."[1]

It is worth noting, in passing, that much uneasiness about the possibility of human consensus arises when-

[1] Bennett Cerf, "Trade Winds," *The Saturday Review of Literature,* February 7, 1949, p. 4.

ever people fail to realize that it is inevitable for them to be at odds in the realm of the inferential. A group will hardly disagree that Adolf Hitler has disappeared from public notice. They will only by the most accidental considerations be together in their assertions as to what happened to him and why.

3. *Statements which refer to what is felt about the situation:* A man not only sees something, he reacts to it; he has sentiments about it as well. He may like, dislike, sympathize, fear, rejoice. He may express disappointment, contempt, anger, pity, enthusiasm, indignation, cynicism, shame. He may be bored, excited, surprised, disturbed, interested. He may feel hopeful, hopeless, resentful, antagonistic. What is said in these moods often reveals little about the housing situation. It tells more about the speakers. They are in effect talking more about what is inside them than about the outside which others can see. What a man feels about something is the product of the countless influences, family, educational, religious, etc., he has been exposed to, shaped by his abilities and purposes. Nevertheless, statements evoked by or expressing these feelings toward the situation may not point to elements in the situation itself.

Leaders are not urged to outlaw these feeling-statements. They are (when possible) to try to move people from an expression of their feelings to a concern with *what* their feelings are about or with the factors in the case which provoked their feelings.

The leader's goal throughout is to get the group to

keep making the first, to recognize the probable and tentative character of the second, and to understand that the third tends to tell more about the speaker than about the facts of the case.

Incidentally, it is difficult to overestimate the value of time given to drill in recognition of these statements. A leader who can spot the character of the talk around the room is abreast of those who get away from the factual. We advise him, however, not to think of himself as a policeman ready to catch infractions. He is rather to play the role of announcer gently calling attention to what others in the heat of talk might forget.

This is followed by a survey of the kinds of problems others have to face. The purpose again is to emphasize the necessity of getting problem-centered. The following is a working classification rather than an exhaustive one.

1. *The Forecaster's Problem.* He must find what is happening so as to predict what will happen. This is the work of the weatherman, the market and investment analyst, the intelligence officer. Without a sharply defined picture of things as they are developing, predictions will be sheerest guesswork.

2. *The Reporter's Problem.* He wishes to be able to tell what happened. He tries to get to the scene of the happening, to go over the ground, to see what he can for himself. He draws on others for background. He calls on all the available witnesses for bits of the story. His

job is to "get the picture," to answer the question "What happened to whom, when and where?" He may be a journalist, a historian, an accountant, a social case worker. The report will be as good as his accuracy, honesty, and coverage.

3. *The Engineer's Problem.* He knows what is wanted. He has the task of finding a way to get it. If a cure for the common cold is the objective, he cannot stop (though he starts) with a description of how and why a cold happens. He is expected to discover the means (i.e., the medicines or regimen) whereby it can be cured. Someone wants a building higher than any other, a wilt-resistant plant, an inexpensive solvent. It is the work of the architect, the agronomist, the chemist to look to the situation and creatively come up with the blueprint, specifications, or formula. This is also the job of the administrator, labor arbitrator, advertising agency, fund-raising committee.

4. *The Judge's Problem.* He is given the laws or rules of the game. His task is to see if in a given case the law was violated and if so to announce the penalty to be paid for the infraction. This is the work of the courts (civil, military, and ecclesiastical), of administrative tribunals, of contest umpires and referees. The facts of the given case constitute the starting point, and the application of the relevant regulation the necessary accompaniment.

5. *The Theorist's Problem.* He has data, scattered, unorganized, unrelated. His task is to build a scheme or conceptual framework which orders and classifies the diversity. Mendelyeev's table showing an "orderly rela-

tionship between the properties of atoms," police reconstructing a crime, Einstein searching for a unitary description to encompass the data of electricity and gravitation, Hans Selye synthesizing the data of bodily reactions in his hypothesis of the general adaptation syndrome—these are examples of theoretical reconstruction. The theorist may, indeed, begin with a grand conception but his work is unfinished until he has learned whether the known data can be included or not.

When we have been able to sensitize a leader to the role of the facts-of-the-case as the necessary base from which discussions proceed, along with some insight as to the kind of statements which veer from the facts, something happens to the leader. He gets a kind of self-assurance not, we think, unrelated to the fact that he has a job to do. He is now a leader with an assignment and a purpose.

You might be surprised (as we were) at the results were you to do all this—just once, even though on reflection you discover that you are simply being urged to heed the old advice about cooking rabbit stew: First catch a hare.

CHAPTER VI

Experience and Innocence

Most of us grow more and more enslaved to the stock conceptions with which we have once become familiar, and less and less capable of assimilating impressions in any but the old ways. Old fogyism, in short, is the inevitable terminus to which life sweeps us on. Objects which violate our established habits of "apperception" are simply not taken account of at all; or, if on some occasion we are forced by dint of argument to admit their existence, twenty-four hours later the admission is as if it were not, and every trace of the unassimilable truth has vanished from our thought. Genius, in truth, means little more than the faculty of perceiving in an unhabitual way. —William James, "Perception," in *The Principles of Psychology,* Henry Holt and Company, 1890, p. 328.

Our problem-minded leader didn't always get the kind of problem-centered discussion he wanted. He might, indeed, succeed in prodding his people away from concern with solutions only to see them bog down on the problem itself.

We located a disturbing factor: a difference of opinion as to the *newness of the problem*. A group, it was observed, will run into trouble if some of the people think in terms of the special features of the problem before them while others see it as something they already know about.

These diverging tendencies had a number of effects. The most immediate was an insistence by some that certain particulars had to be taken into account, while others argued that they ought to get to the answers because the main outlines of the problem were already understood. We came to interpret this as a clash between the Innocents and the Experienced, that is, between those who were oriented in the present and those who took their experience with similar situations in the past as a point of departure.

A team of observers (usually three) was used in studying this phenomenon.

Attempts to estimate the degree of orientation around each of these perspectives were fruitless. No measure could be devised which gave even a rough agreement as to how much "uniqueness thinking" was being shown. (We also gave up the attempt to catalogue the forms which the disagreement took. The classifications led to some fancy nomenclature but no new insight on the process. We are content to believe that recognition of the divergence is more important than a listing of its varieties.) We found, however, that observers could get together when they were set to chart the tendency rather than the amount. The tendencies were defined this way.

The Innocent	The Experienced
He wants to talk about the particulars in the problem before the group.	He wants to use the solution which worked before on a similar problem.
He wants to see the problem in the special way it arose and in terms of its special effects.	He is impatient with the desire to spend more time on the uniqueness of the problem because he feels that the experience of the past will apply now.
He wants a solution to fit the unique characteristics of this problem as it exists now.	He believes that if a procedure worked in a comparable situation it will work well enough in this one.

Then Mr. Turner had an idea. He was head of a social agency doing an admittedly good job in a large city. He met with his staff of eleven once a week for talk about policies and plans. He was giving a certain amount of time to setting up groups of volunteer friends of the agency. He hoped they would build enough *esprit* to work on their own without so much calling on him and his subordinates for instructions.

He thought our studies might help. We, at least, were able to use his groups for our probings.

That, however, isn't the point of the story. During one of our conversations Mr. Turner wondered about the meetings of his own staff. It was his impression that his people were well trained, loyal, and eager to do a good job, but they were not getting as much done in their weekly sessions as they should. Too many matters had to be carried over. And would I care to bring my pad and pencil to his staff meeting?

After the third session he and I agreed that he had almost a laboratory specimen of the innocence-experience difficulty. Four of his staff were "smart old hands" with much background in agency work. Three others were equally smart but with fewer years in this business. They were more likely to want to start from scratch on problems. The remaining four were middle-of-the-roaders. When something came up the talk was lively and relevant. But the split in their philosophies was very much in evidence. The talk swirled around the two positions: "We need a way to get at *this* thing"—"Let's do it the way we did it before."

It seemed clear that this way of tackling an issue not only was time-wasting but kept members from realizing the wisdom that was in the group. If there was something new in a problem situation, then it needed attention. If the situation had elements in it which could be dealt with by old procedures, then they must not be slighted. There was need, in short, of a kind of unifying perspective by which to capture and amalgamate the old and the new, the particular and the similar. There was need of a device by which to exploit George Santayana's insight that "Those who cannot remember the past are condemned to repeat it," and Winston Churchill's that "Past experience carries with its advantage the drawback that things never happen the same way again."

G. B. Shaw gave us a point of view. He said, "The only man who behaves sensibly is my tailor; he takes my measure anew every time he sees me, whilst all the rest go on with their old measurements, and expect them to fit me."

This puts the issue in actional terms. Do the old measurements fit? If they do, it is surely unwise to change them. If they do not, it is equally unwise to preserve them.

But what to do?

It was doubtful if anything could be done to change the attitudes of the seven non-middle-of-the-road staff members. They seemed too deeply canalized. Could anything be done to reroute their tendencies, so as to head off the philosophical conflict?

Mr. Turner then had his idea. "Why don't we handle our problems in case fashion, the way our social workers do? What would happen if each of our big problems was put as a case?"

On the face of it this meant that any matter had to be thought about in narrative rather than in question or statement form. Now the problem would not be a question to be debated, but rather a concrete and particular situation described in a context of details. A group, in short, would not be presented with an issue without an accompanying story in connection with which the question was to be asked. Mr. Turner thought that once the case was on the table people would be more likely to look to it than to their differences about "newness" or "oldness." That is to say, the disturbing conclusions about the nature of the problem might be deflected for a time as attention was focused on the problem itself. It was their secondary judgment about the uniqueness which led to trouble, not the matter itself.

Thus, if the people could be forced to hold the secondary attitudes in abeyance, maybe they'd be able to take the measurements of the problem.

An instruction sheet was devised. At the end of the next staff meeting Mr. Turner very gently requested their coöperation on a small experiment. Would they come to the next meeting ready to talk in a rather organized way about the important issues which came up? Would they in the meantime study this form?

Staff-Meeting Procedure

I. State a case as the basis for any decision. A case is a story of some situation which you wish to call attention to or which you want to do something about.

   A. Do not say "We need more workers in District 8."

Do tell us what is happening in District 8, what is or is not being accomplished. Give the background story before you give the summary and your conclusion.

B. Do not be concerned if this takes more time. If your knowledge of the situation is set out first, the group will better understand your interest in the situation.

II. The person who presented the case is then available for questions so as to insure understanding of what was said.

III. The case is now to be considered the business of the group. Addition and amplification of details, and amendments or modifications are in order.

IV. Recommendations for necessary action. Members are to withhold recommendations until requested by the chairman.

Mr. Turner spent the opening ten minutes of the next session reviewing the volume of old and new business on his agenda. He was sure the staff had some items he didn't know about. He was a bit worried lest they fall behind. He was proposing this "new" procedure as an experiment to be used only if it worked. If it proved unsatisfactory he would be the first to urge its abandonment. He hoped they would give it a try. In order to get under way he would state in case form an urgent request from L— House for the immediate establishment of . . .

The statement took five and a half minutes. He invited questions. They took fourteen minutes. Only one comment using forty-five seconds was made in Step III. Recommendations and a decision were made in six minutes.

Was roughly thirty minutes too much or too little to give to this matter? There is now no way of knowing because no basis of comparison exists. Some things are known: There seemed to be no waste motion. The direction of the talk was clearly defined. The staff members knew when they were finished. The innocence-experience difficulty hardly emerged. Was it because of the character of the problem or because it was headed off? We know only that nothing encouraged its appearance. The members were literally forced to focus on Mr. Turner's case.

It took a while before the staff learned to think in case terms. A few thought the procedure might be time-consuming. But even they confessed that they could see advantages in starting with a case. Everybody had a chance to get on the same communication line at the outset. The innocence-experience difficulty was not dissolved. Even in the ninth meeting with the new procedure an observer could chart the seven— but it was not so easy as before. The manifestations were by no means so overt.

The story method is not proposed as a cure-all. It is simply a device by which to force all members of a group to become creatively problem-conscious at the same time. We think of it as a kind of protection against the intrusion of secondary conflict-arousing judgments. These still arise in groups who use the case procedure. But they arise in circumstances where they look out of place. By the time the first two steps have been covered the impulse to think that the problem is an old or a new one is dissipated or stripped of its relevance. And the real marvel is that the people occasionally recognize that this impulse is out of place, that in the end it is the resolution of the problem that is important, not the determination of the problem's newness or oldness.

The procedure is not to be looked upon as any radical departure from ordinarily effective practice. The only thing to be urged here is that it may help to make such practice explicit. When a group has learned to feel comfortable with it their talking takes on a new quality. It becomes more organized, more to the point. It is doubtful whether any theoretical consideration of this can be as convincing as a demonstration.

Incidentally, in every one of Mr. Turner's newly organized voluntary groups the "procedure" is the first item of business.

CHAPTER VII

The Problem of the Partisan

. . . Wear not, there, one mood only in thyself;
think not that thy word, and thine alone, must be
right. For, if any man thinks that he alone is wise,—
that in speech, or in mind, he hath no peer,—such a
soul, when laid open, is ever found empty. No,
though a man be wise 'tis no shame for him to learn
many things, and to bend in season. —Haemon in
Sophocles' *Antigone.*

Nicholas Murray Butler: "The name of a notable
historic family, the house of Bourbon, has passed into
familiar speech with the definition of one who forgets
nothing and who learns nothing. The Bourbon typifies
the closed mind."

Samuel Johnson: "It is a very good custom to keep
a journal for a man's own use; he may write upon a
card a day all that is necessary to be written, after he
has had experience of life. At first there is a great deal
to be written, because there is a great deal of novelty;

81

but when a man once has settled his opinions, there is seldom much to be set down."

Lincoln Steffens: "If you know too surely, you cannot learn; and for the purpose of research, you may have theories, but never, never knowledge."

Heywood Broun: "Once a man takes sides he begins to see a little less of the world."

Such statements are part of an intellectual tradition in which there is defined the phenomenon of the partisan—the man whose focus is fixed and whose view of the world is firmly organized.

The partisan is so much a part of the discussion scene that we studied him both as a specimen and as a symptom of the problems of human discord. What is he like? What does he do when he is most troublesome?

In the simplest terms he was (1) persistent and (2) partial.

His persistence ranged all the way from a repetition of his position, through an insistence that it had to be given attention, to the assertion that there was no other. At the outset this by itself was considered the bothersome factor, but after a while we saw that it was an inevitable part of any effort to get things done. Wasn't persistence, after all, a sign of a good worker, doing what he had to do? The more he kept after what he needed the more likely he was to get it. Haven't we all listened to speeches on the connection between perseverance and success? Do not the pages of biography glow with the feats of endurance and stick-to-it-iveness of the Ehrlichs, Curies, Burbanks, Edisons? After considerable cataloguing of the habits of persistent people we abandoned this lead.

We then looked to the "partial" factor. And here, we think, we found something. The partisan, in our view, was a person who saw only a bit of the problem. He was a man on one *side* with a set of restricted interests. He tended to see the situation in the focus of his purposes.

In a sense, of course, everyone is a partisan. Who is there who sees all, knows all? Each of us sees only an arc of a great circle. Where is the man who is not selective and specialized in his interests?

But there are levels of partisanship. Some tongues taste more. The child sees less than the sophisticated adult. The experts catch what the untrained miss. Those who stay and listen hear more than those who leave.

The Partisan and the Administrator

This perspective on levels gave us a way of thinking about an enduring difficulty—the relations between an administrator and his operating assistants. Let us consider this the prototype of the partisan problem.

If an organization had enough space, equipment, funds, and personnel to satisfy the demands of everyone, the administrator would have little to do. His work really begins when an assistant asks for more than he is given.

Listen in on a plant manager (or general or dean or bishop or union president or anyone high in an organizational hierarchy) talking to a lower-echelon head about something the latter wants. The drama of their discussion unfolds around a conflict of interests.

The Partisan	*The Administrator*
He sees the needs of his department.	He sees the needs of the other departments as well.
He wants to take care of his men.	He has to take care of all the men.
He wants peace, convenience, and efficiency where he works.	He must keep peace all over the plant.
He has his problem to solve.	He must see that solving one problem does not create others.

The partisan is oriented around the small circle of his needs; the administrator around the circles of his several assistants. This departmental selfishness may be deplored in the abstract but on the level of action it is inevitable. A section head without loyalty to the demands of those with whom he works is also without the means of arousing their allegiance in the work they must do. Unless he identifies himself with his men why should they "go all out" for him?

The administrator who loses his larger perspective is necessarily open to the dangers of favoritism and incompleteness in his allegiance.

Can the gulf between the administrator and his subordinates be bridged?

The Goal

In the course of observations we recognized at least nine possible outcomes of talk when partisans meet.

1. A *solution* emerges which satisfies everyone so that each gets exactly what he wants.

2. A *satisfactory adjustment* is reached whereby each gains his central or major objective, i.e., essentially what he is after.

3. A *compromise settlement* comes after negotiation and mutual concession. This is the result of a kind of barter in which each "yields something for the sake of receiving something."

4. A *resolution by reason* comes about when one man is shown that his position is untenable because his statements about the facts were false, his picture of the situation was incomplete, or his conclusions could not be supported without violating the criteria of evidence. When the partisan is thus shown the inadequacy of his position and when he assents to it without loss of face the problem vanishes.

5. A *decision is imposed* by one group in a discus-

sion because it has the strength in numbers or status to do so and because it is unwilling to recognize any legitimacy in the claims of the other. The conflict is thus dodged, suppressed, or postponed, but not eliminated so long as the minority or weaker group remains on the ground.

6. A *surrender* results when one of the partisans becomes weary of the talk, when he feels the futility of ever getting his views appreciated. He gives up in the face of sustained resistance not because of any feeling that his (or his group's) needs and desires are unjustified but because he has lost the will to present his case. This is decision by attrition. Since it is one-sided, it, too, postpones rather than settles the issue.

7. A *withdrawal* is made by one of the contestants, who, as a result of a fraudulent statement of the case, has been persuaded that he will suffer if he gets what he wants. This is the public counterpart of a confidence game and peace prevails so long as the duped party is unaware of what happened. This mode of resolution resembles 4 but the consequences, if the duplicity is revealed, are considerably different.

8. A *sellout* occurs when one of the participants gives up his battle for the need of his group to accept some personal advantage from another participant. The person thus bribed may then retain his status as representative for his men if he can satisfy them that he has actually acted in their behalf. Failing that, he

is usually replaced, unless he resorts to force or more fraud to keep his position.

9. A *stalemate* is reached when there is neither the strength or wish to surrender on the one hand nor the will to compromise and adjustment on the other.

The strategy is now clear: the object of talk is to do everything to avoid a stalemate and to promote the achievement of 1, 2, or 3 rather than 5, 6, 7, or 8. The choice is against the latter on grounds of justice and effect. They are unfair and they leave the source of the difficulty untouched.

How does one go about promoting the achievement of 1, 2, or 3? What activity or training can a partisan or administrator undertake which will encourage that? We experimented with a number of procedures. None worked. It does not even seem worth while to describe these failures.

Why Compromise?

There was one by-product of this effort, nevertheless, which deserves attention. It was standard practice to discuss our theories and experiments with the members of each group after we had observed them. While on this partisan problem we were moved to analyze our conversations on the role of compromise. One fact stood out: Ever so many people either distrusted or had reservations about it. Few came out with a strong defense of it. Only twice in twenty-one such conversations did someone say that "people ought to learn the values of compromise."

We were somewhat astonished to learn that "compromise" was a word with unpleasant associations.

We heard arguments like these:

"If you show that you are willing to give ground they'll take it as a sign of weakness and then they'll argue for what they want harder than ever."

"Anybody willing to compromise really doesn't have the courage of his convictions. If you don't believe in yourself no one will. So you have to sit tight."

"Compromise is appeasement. Remember Chamberlain? He gave an inch and then Hitler kept on 'til he went after a mile."

"Sure I'm willing to give and take. But how do I know about the other fellow? Why doesn't he make me an offer? Why should I make the first move?"

"I don't see why I should want less than I want. I think I'm justified or I wouldn't ask for it. I'm not in any gyp business. Suppose I am a storekeeper. If my price is right why should I change it?"

If the attitudes which usually accompany such statements are at all strong, it is not surprising if the talk ends in stalemate. Indeed, in our experience these statements usually announce the end of discussion, or at least the end of progress to any settlement.

Incidentally, these people were echoing a point of view which can be found elsewhere.

Stuart Chase: "If an American says, 'Let's compromise the matter,' a Russian is deeply shocked. 'Compromise' to him does not mean friendly, fair negotiation, but an abject surrender of principle and the lowest kind of conniving rascality. Americans catch a hint of his feeling in their phrase 'a compromised woman.' To a Russian this is the only meaning."[1]

Ralph Waldo Emerson: "Every compromise was surrender and invited new demands."[2]

Charles Sumner: "From the beginning of our history the country has been afflicted with compromise. It is by compromise that human rights have been abandoned. I insist that this shall cease. The country needs repose after all its trials; it deserves repose. And repose can only be found in everlasting principles."

Tryon Edwards: "Compromise is but the sacrifice of one right or good in the hope of retaining another, too often ending in the loss of both."

Witnesses to another point of view could also be found:

John Herman Randall, Jr.: "Now anybody who is at all capable of learning anything from experience knows that the only way to get along with people, the only way to do anything together with anybody else, is through compromise. You don't need exceptional brains to realize that; you need only to be married or to have a friend. Coöperation between human beings

[1] "Danger: Men Talking," *This Week Magazine*, March 5, 1950, pp. 5 and 18.

[2] Unless otherwise indicated these "Quotes on Compromise" are from *The New York Times Magazine*, January 19, 1947, p. 6.

is possible only if they are willing to compromise; and politics, the art of coöperation, of group action, is at bottom nothing but the practical application of the method of compromise."[3]

Edmund Burke: "All government,—indeed every human benefit and enjoyment, every virtue and every prudent act,—is founded on compromise and barter."

Samuel Johnson: "Life cannot subsist in society but by reciprocal concessions."

William Shakespeare: "What you cannot as you would achieve, you must perforce accomplish as you may."

How can this be? How can such shrewd observers come to such varying views? Remember the doctrine of Chapter IV? Our hunch is that they are catching up in the word "compromise" quite different items. Those who have no confidence in the process are referring, we think, to the surrender-imposed-manipulated-sort-of-settlements summarized in 5, 6, 7, and 8 above. Those who see merit in the process have in mind the negotiations summarized in 1, 2, and 3 between men equal in strength or disposed to work things out to mutual rather than private advantage.

How can partisans in discussion be helped to discover the attitudes which will make them ready to give and take? I have no answer or advice but this:

[3] "On the Importance of Being Unprincipled," *The American Scholar*, Spring, 1938, pp. 132–133.

They ought first to be reminded that a compromise settlement is a decent, honorable, and useful demonstration of practical intelligence. Then, their attention ought to be called to the varieties of settlement which are one-sided and which they ought to distrust. Much is accomplished if a leader can be persuaded to say these things out loud. The direct affirmation of the values of "honest" compromise (i.e., as we have defined it in 3) is itself a large step in a group. It is a guiding principle for the uncertain, and thus-oriented members of a group are often disposed to search willingly for a compromise without the weakness or stigma that is supposed to go with it.

It needs to be said that compromise is not an easy accomplishment when a partisan is weak. As Dean Inge put it, "It is useless for the sheep to pass resolutions in favor of vegetarianism, while the wolf remains of a different opinion." When the strong (or the dishonest) take over, discussion is stultified.

There is a very real danger that, whenever the fear of submission and manipulation is strong, the urge to obduracy will also deepen. Then men become unwilling and afraid to use their intelligence to work things out. This is the mood in which partisans yield to the urge to fight it out. When the will to turn from a synthesis of desires to a power struggle has emerged it is then of little use to talk about the values of talking together. We must, nevertheless, not be resigned to the inevitability of this kind of defeat. Though it may come in spite of our urging, we are, in the interests of human concord, bound at least to resist it.

David E. Lilienthal said it better:

One of the most beautiful phrases in our language are the words an American uses when he says to those with whom he has been in disagreement: "I'll go along with you. That's not the way I see it, but I'll go along." Out of this precept of reasonableness and respect for the opinions of others often issues one of the finest fruits of thought: a composite judgment, the product of many minds.

The considered judgment of men who reason together embodies more than "tolerance," which is, after all, a somewhat thin and negative concept. It is rather based on an affirmative belief in the value of blending diverse experiences, diverse backgrounds. Such a composite or group judgment can be sturdier than any one of the individual judgments that make it up. This harmonizing of conflicting views into a common conclusion is not merely the trader's "splitting the difference"; it is not compromise for its own sake. It is a doctrine in exact contradiction to the growing fanaticism and dogmatism in the world, in which differences from an official party line are dealt with as traitorous and in which the accommodation of conflicting ideas is regarded as a sign of weakness rather than what it is in fact: a mark of strength.[4]

[4] *This I Do Believe*, Harper & Brothers, 1949, pp. 35–36.

CHAPTER VIII

Making Phrases at Each Other

Harry Hershfield tells of a cop who clubbed a spectator at a parade, calling him a Communist. "But I'm an anti-Communist!" the spectator protested. "I don't care what kind of a Communist you are!" said the cop. "Get outa here!" —Earl Wilson, *The New York Post*, April 16, 1948, p. 52.

One of the tantalizing phenomena of the discussion process is the "stopper." Men go along easily, asserting, questioning, denying. Then, someone says or does something. There is a moment of uncertainty. The talk stops. The talk picks up again, but it is off the track. It wanders. The men have lost direction. They fumble a bit. Sometimes they get back on the track. Sometimes they don't.

Some stoppers:

- A man reminisces about something only dimly related to the subject at hand; when he is finished no one quite knows what the point was.

- Two or three pursue some topic by themselves as if they were alone in the room; then they are noticed.
- A man gets wound up, going on and on until the others lose interest. He stops and no one knows where to begin.
- One man insults another or the group.
- A man loses his head and talks wildly. His listeners' sympathy is mixed with embarrassment.
- A man gets off the subject and another tells him about it. The issue is a new one: is he on the subject?

These stoppers seem violations of the common courtesies, demonstrations of what used to be called bad manners. This is not the place for an analysis of the means of correcting them.

But there is one stopper that we have tried to do something about, probably because it seemed to have nothing in common with the others. It is the "stigma."

A man describes a situation, takes a position, or makes a proposal. A listener says:

"But that's _____!"

"Why that is nothing but _____!"

"You're proposing _____!"

"Jim, you are a _____!"

"A clear example of _____!"

"Well, of course, they're _____!"

Substitute for the blank any word or phrase used in connection with something considered undesirable— any one of these, for example: un-American, fascist, communist, socialism, New Dealer, capitalist, Wall

Street lackey, conservative, reactionary, fundamental-
ist, radical, drunkard, thief, liar, delinquent, coward,
childish, fool, politician, demagogue, warmonger, pac-
ifist, militarist, a racket, appeasement, fifth columnist,
Quisling . . .

The first speaker is now identified with the stigma.
Sometimes it stops him cold. Sometimes he denies its
relevance. Sometimes he finds a stigma for his listener.
The talk turns on the implication of the stigma. The
subject fades away.

The Stigma: Its Use and Abuse

A word becomes a stigma by a process both histori-
cal and psychological. For our purposes a rather simple
theory of the stigma's functioning may be enough. It
begins with the notion that words go with or reflect
attitudes or feelings.

Every minute of every waking hour a man has some
sort of awareness, some feelings or attitudes. These
awarenesses shift rapidly or one may persist or several
may blend—but let a man be alive and awake and he
will feel something. He may be pleased, frightened,
angry, satisfied, surprised, ashamed, bored, tired, disgruntled, comfortable, in pain, hopeful, despairing,
forgiving, ambitious, numb, excited, dizzy, resigned,
confident, pitying, sorrowful, aghast, wondering, ada-
mant, worshipful, cynical, optimistic, pessimistic, ex-
pectant, eager, uncertain, assured, uneasy, happy, ter-
rified—the list of possible feelings is a long one.

It matters little whether they be classified one way

or another. In one catch-all view these feelings can be arranged in this form:

The pain-ful, disap-proving, un-comfortable, negative, despairing	The mildly painful, etc.	The indif-ferent or in-explicit	The mildly pleasant, etc.	The pleas-ant, approv-ing, com-fortable, positive, hopeful

Suppose, further, that every expression of a man's relationship with a thing, person, or situation will involve some feeling to it, which feeling will be reflected or involved in what he says.

The senator is in front of the audience for thirty minutes. At the end three people comment:

A: "Mere rhetoric and bombast."

B: "He spoke about foreign affairs and the audience clapped hands for five minutes when he finished."

C: "Eloquence and great speaking."

After questioning the three further, an interviewer is assured that the feeling in A was disapproval, in B indifference, in C approval.

The same word can be used in settings which reflect different feelings. Three people are referring to three different men:

A: "He is a bastard."

B: "He is a bastard."

C: "He is a bastard."

In the particular settings it is found that the feeling in A is one of disapproval, that the man was born out of wedlock; in B the feeling is of indifference, the speaker wishing only to distinguish the birth from one when the parents are married; in C at the beer party one lodge brother refers in friendly fashion to another.

Any word in English, then, may be used as a *stigma* when the feeling involves disapproval or negativeness, as an *inexplicit* term when the feeling is one of unconcern or non-interest, and as a *halo* when the feeling involves approval or positiveness. In short, a word has a stigma- or halo-function only when somebody uses or takes it so.

Most of the time this is no conscious, deliberate process. A person doesn't sit back and say to himself, "I want to say something about the proposal just advanced. I feel negative about it. What is a good word to express my attitude so the others will know I don't like the proposal?" Something like that may happen, but for the most part one has at hand a vocabulary organized and ready for this kind of evaluative indication.

There is nothing intrinsic in a word that makes us use it for either approval or disapproval. Custom is a sufficient explanation. Though each of us develops his own ways of characterization there are broad tendencies in our usage. When Jon Stone said that it was "damned nonsense," his hearers could assume with considerable assurance that he was not expressing approval. When a man was referred to as an "infamous impostor" it is likely that that phrase reflected feelings different from those involved when he was called a "prophet, seer, and revelator"—even though on occasion a man might have contrary feelings and use these words in an ironic or just nonconventional way.

That usage does become established is rather well revealed in Ben W. Palmer's illustration. Do you have any doubt which terms you would choose if you liked or disliked the President?

The President achieved $\frac{\text{notoriety}}{\text{fame}}$ by $\frac{\text{stubbornly, bit-}}{\text{tenaciously, vig-}}$ $\frac{\text{terly, fanatically}}{\text{orously, zealously}}$ asserting his $\frac{\text{impudent pretensions}}{\text{bold claims}}$ even in legislative councils through his $\frac{\text{tools}}{\text{agents}}$ who $\frac{\text{cunningly}}{\text{skillfully}}$ $\frac{\text{insinuated}}{\text{introduced}}$ themselves into those councils. The Senate being in accord with his $\frac{\text{prejudices}}{\text{principles}}$ $\frac{\text{succumbed}}{\text{yielded}}$ to his $\frac{\text{domination.}}{\text{leadership.}}$ He was a man of $\frac{\text{superstition}}{\text{faith}}$ and of $\frac{\text{obsti-}}{\text{strength}}$ $\frac{\text{nacy}}{\text{of purpose}}$ whose policy combined $\frac{\text{bigotry and arrogance}}{\text{firmness and courage}}$ with $\frac{\text{cowardice.}}{\text{caution.}}$

He was a $\frac{\text{creature}}{\text{man}}$ of strong $\frac{\text{biases}}{\text{convictions}}$ and belonged in the camp of the $\frac{\text{reactionaries.}}{\text{conservatives.}}$ His conduct of the presidency $\frac{\text{portended}}{\text{foreshadowed}}$ a $\frac{\text{degeneration}}{\text{change}}$ of that office into one of $\frac{\text{dictatorship.}}{\text{leadership.}}$[1]

If talking necessarily involves naming people and actions and indicating how the talker feels about them, what does this have to do with discussion?

There is nothing about a stigma word as such which leads to trouble. It is as necessary a phase of the talk process as the halo or inexplicit term. Nevertheless, when a man is moved to stigmatize a person or situation or argument, in our experience the result very often is a dramatic dead end. Once something is stigmatized it tends to be located and fixed. A barrier is set up around it and further discussion is shunted away. It is as if the speaker said, "Nothing can be said further. I've catalogued the thing and there is no other way to do it."

A staff had considered hiring a research agency to survey job assignments. There were pros and cons. Then Jon Stone said, "They're a bunch of racketeers." Somehow this "fixed" the issue. An anti-Stoneite could reply, "No, they are not. They're an honest outfit." But the barrier was up. The agency was tagged. And it was not easy to get out from under the influence of the stigma. It was like an umbrella which kept men from seeing the heavens beyond.

Organizations at work on behalf of "the handi-

[1] *American Bar Association Journal*, July, 1949, p. 559.

capped," those released from "insane asylums," "juvenile delinquents," "epileptics," "lepers" have had to fight long and hard against the imprisoning effects of the stigma. People seem stopped by the label from looking beyond it to what it points to. Though an epileptic is thoroughly normal when he is not having a seizure, and a man released from a leper colony is by no means dangerous, it still takes a strong sort of evaluating penetration to see beyond the feeling of suspicion derived from negative associations with the words.

What Dr. William Alanson White wrote in connection with physicians fits here: "Giving something a name seems to have a deadening influence upon all our relations to it. It brings matters to a finality. Nothing further seems to need to be done. The disease has been identified. The necessity for further understanding of it has ceased to exist. And so classifications . . . had a sterilizing effect upon further inquiries."[2]

Again it should be said, the stigma word is inevitable and unavoidable. To outlaw it would be to prevent the expression of a tremendous area of human concern. Would it be humanly possible to stop people from saying they dislike something? Would you want to?

There would be values, however, in a tactic by

[2] William A. White, *William Alanson White: The Autobiography of a Purpose*, Doubleday & Company, 1938, p. 53.

which a group could be sensitized to the stigma's dead-end effect.

We have found but one way to get at it. We work through the leader. He is urged to recognize that

- A stigma word may well be an accurate indication of how someone feels about a person or situation.
- A stigma word describes a situation from a particular point of view. It applies to an aspect of things as one person sees it. It is a fractional indicator. Every name gets to a bit of something, not all of it.
- A stigma word may put a brake on further discussion of an issue. This is the danger the leader must watch for. Should a stigma word be an invitation to more scrutiny on the issue, then it is to be welcomed. When it limits analysis or cuts off consideration, then its braking influence must be exposed.

What should a leader do when the stopper is at work? He is urged to say something like

- "The gentleman said 'the agency is a racket!' That is certainly one way of looking at it. Is there any other?"
- "Certainly Mr. Stone's feeling about the agency is clear. Does it exhaust what can be said about it?"
- "Mr. Stone has pegged the agency. Is that true all the time. Is it always that?"

This direct attack by the leader on the stigma does not guarantee that the limiting effects will be removed. But it does invite and encourage more talk. If it doesn't remove the effect, it undercuts it. In groups where the leader or anyone else does something similar the uncertainty and stoppage of talk are less apparent. Under the prodding of his question the talk usually starts again. When he has spotted stigmas long enough, he may even find that the practice is picked up by others.

CHAPTER IX

"A Shy, Socratic Approach"

The little word *my* is the most important one in all human affairs and properly to reckon with it is the beginning of wisdom. It has the same force whether it is *my* dinner, *my* dog, and *my* house, or *my* faith, *my* country and *my* God. We not only resent the imputation that our watch is wrong, or our car shabby, but that our conception of the canals of Mars, of the pronunciation of "Epictetus," of the medicinal value of salicine, or the date of Sargon I, are subject to revision. —James Harvey Robinson, *Mind in the Making*, Harper & Brothers, 1921, p. 44.

Once I took a clinical psychologist to a meeting of nine men and five women assigned the task of approving a new course of study in a large school system. Seven were heads of departments and seven teachers in other departments. The fourteen represented about 300 faculty members.

After the meeting I asked the psychologist to comment on my analysis of the activities of the leader. He didn't want to do that. He thought something else important. What follows is a free translation of what he said. After reading it he said, "It has the substance of my views, but it is so brief that it may oversimplify the difficulty I was getting at. If a reader bears that in mind I'll OK it."

You must give some attention to the personality structure of these people. Let's talk in nontechnical language. Somewhere along the line, your people have to learn something about the nature of their reactions to each other. If what we heard this evening is typical of what usually goes on, then you have to think about the way in which these people take criticism. Did you see that man's defensiveness when the younger woman attacked his schedule? His actions just happened to be more violent and overt than those of the others. Pick up a textbook in mental hygiene or abnormal or social psychology[1] and read about "defense mechanisms." I'm very sure you will find that the classic

[1] People commonly become defensive when attitudes which are important to them are challenged. They quite literally act as though they are defending something which belongs to them. If a man's beliefs as a Roman Catholic or as a political liberal, for example, are questioned, he is very likely to feel that something important is being undermined. It is not only his church or his political associates which are being attacked, but also he himself. And so he is likely to respond with expressions of hurt feelings or with counterattack. When heated remarks are made in the course of a political argument, for example, the participants are not merely seeking to convince each other of something. Each is also defending himself against the implied accusation that he is somehow unworthy or mistaken. The heat with which the argument is carried on is best explained as counterattack in the face of threat. Theodore M. Newcomb, *Social Psychology*, The Dryden Press, 1950, p. 248.

symptoms were well pictured this evening. In fact, you should be able to document the textbook at many points with illustrations from what you saw in the committee. I'm also sure that the way these people took criticism affected their thinking about the course of study. When a person feels attacked, he stops listening and works twice as hard to justify his position. If a man has a sense of his own inferiority, and if someone questions a point he makes, he is driven to emphasize the soundness of what he said with more than customary vigor. He then stops his study of the problem. It takes a person in fine balance, in good adjustment to look at criticism objectively. Anybody with less balance tends to take criticism as a threat to his standing in the group. You surely understand that what I am talking about is a widely accepted analysis of a certain kind of adjustment. This is my conclusion: Either the members of that group need some kind of instruction on how to look at their defense mechanisms, or you have to find a way of teaching them how to criticize each other without touching on their feelings of inferiority.

Before letting him go I sought his reaction to another way of explaining the problem. He is not responsible for this view:

However it happens, a man sees a situation in his own personal way. He has conclusions about it and maybe some theory about how to deal with it. He works this all over inside himself. It is his creation. He puts his notions in words. He tells others about them. He now has created two things: the notions inside him and the statement which others heard. These are his progeny. They belong to him. He identifies himself with them. And if someone attacks an argument based on his notions he sees it as an attack on himself. Our man has thus personalized the criticism process. He has not learned to see the difference between (1) a criticism directed to an argument and (2) a criticism directed to an opponent. Perhaps the psychologist's inferiority-defensiveness theory can explain why our man doesn't see the distinction. Let me take refuge in a teacher's position and say only that he doesn't make the distinction because he has never learned how to make it. No one ever helped him face the fact he now doesn't see. Cannot a man learn to hold off resentment when another questions an argument, if that other man had no intention of attacking the maker of the argument? Can you not learn to see that you are making an inference if you say that another's differing with your statements involves also an attempt to discredit you? If it can be shown that the man across the room is trying to ridicule you, hold you in contempt before the group, then your attempt to retaliate or justify yourself makes sense. But when you start by assuming that every doubt about what you say inevitably carries with it an attempt to stigmatize you, and when you overlook that assumption, then your behavior makes less sense. I admit that it is much easier for me to identify myself with what I say than it is to stand off and consider what I say apart from the fact that I said it. But can one not learn to stand off so?

Let me put this in another way. Suppose I study an object. I tell you what I see. What I say can range all the way from the accurate, precise, and detailed to the false, ambiguous, and vague. Let's say that my description is unclear on some point. You note that. You may have no purpose other than to get the thing clear. If I now go beyond that to believe you are ridiculing me, then what is called "sensitiveness to criticism" looks like a manifestation of my assumption-making. I admit that there is cogency in your saying that it "looks like a manifestation of my inferiority feelings." But remember that I am offering another theory, not trying to deny yours. And, please, my not staying with your theory involves no criticism of you as a person.

This argument is not a new one. Students of argumentation and logic have long been distinguishing between an argument *ad rem* and an argument *ad hominem*. The first is on the issue, the second on the character and motives of the opposition. Am I just riding a hobby if I believe that one *can* differ with an analysis of the *rem* without even thinking of the purposes and intelligence of the *hominem*?

Of course, my friend saw less merit in my theory than in his, and vice versa. But that does not mean that either of us must be attacking the other as a person. We differ and we know it. Each sees what he sees. Each creates what he creates.

An Approach to Criticism

Instead of wondering about our personal adequacy and using up good time about it, and instead of arguing about the validity of each theory, it seemed wise to ask, What action does each theory lead to? What can men in a group do with it?

As a way of getting to these questions an investigation was devised along this line: What happens when criticism is taken? Is there anything a person does which deflects the feeling of defensiveness in another? Does all talk in criticism have the same form? Is there any way of getting *ad rem* without another's assuming you are being *ad hominem?*

Observers were set to isolating critical interchanges which did and did not give rise to feelings of defensiveness. We looked at dozens of these. Leaders of groups were interviewed for their experiences with this phenomenon. Suggestions came from twenty-two which were helpful. We began to discern an "aggressiveness quotient." Some approaches to criticism seemed to stir things up, ruffle feelings faster. Some seemed more conciliatory.

What we were getting was again part of the experience of others. T. H. Pear had written about this a dozen years earlier.

In some social groups there is the convention that when any one breaks in upon a speaker, to differ with him, the form of interruption should mention the other one's name or title, if the speaker's relationship is distant, and use a term of familiarity, endearment, or affectionate insult if it is intimate. After this there often follows a gentle phrase, the choice of which may even characterize the interrupter's social group. "I wonder if I might? . . ." "Don't you think it's just possible to look at that in another way? . . ." "I shouldn't dream of contradicting you—but I used to live with these people. . . ." "Aren't you forgetting that their point of view may be caused by the way they have suffered lately? . . ." "Of course, tastes differ, but I shouldn't feel honest if I didn't say. . . ." etc. Some readers may think that all these phrases are insincere, and that "I don't agree" is enough; that if you think the other man a fool or a liar you ought not to suffer him gladly. Yet "he who says what he likes, will soon hear something he doesn't," is not a bad motto of social life. Indeed, people whose job requires them to be unusually polite, in circumstances where incivility would lead to failure or even dismissal, learn many pleasant and not always insincere phrases, and, like a tennis player, choose their strokes for the occasion.[2]

Almost everything we found supported Pear's conclusion about the use of "a gentle phrase." The broadest generalization that might be made is this: A man's resistance to criticism will be inversely proportional to the critic's assurance that he is not trying to show his superiority by making the criticism.

This sounds too conclusive. In terms of our actual findings it is little more than a working hypothesis. But it was a suggestive one. What would happen if we tried to persuade people to preface every statement of any disagreement with some kind of soft approach deliberately designed to keep the listener's inferiority from being tapped?

The officer in charge of research in the school system was eager to go along with a proposal to set up a

[2] T. H. Pear, *The Maturing Mind*, Thomas Nelson and Sons, 1938, pp. 83–84.

pilot study on group methods with the seven teachers who were on the curriculum committee. Five of them were able to meet with ten others from other committees. We had nine two-hour sessions. Lectures alternated with demonstrations. Whatever was proposed as theoretically useful was tried out in practice situations in the group. Three of the nine sessions were given over to the "prevention of defensivenss." Only seven of the teachers were told about the business of "a gentle phrase." They met apart from the remainder, who with another instructor worked on some other aspects of talking together. The seven split into two groups, one demonstrating while the other observed. After the three meetings we were satisfied that they knew what we were after. The following bit about Mrs. Eleanor Roosevelt's behavior as a United Nations delegate served as a model:

Mrs. Roosevelt has, moreover, polished to a high degree an effective method of debating that comes naturally to her but of the value of which experience has made her thoroughly aware—a shy, Socratic approach to the matter at hand. In an arena dominated by men who seem to have made up their minds, she goes out of her way not to appear opinionated, even though her own mind may be pretty well made up, too. "Now, of course, I'm a woman and I don't understand all these things," she will remark softly, almost maternally, "and I'm sure there's a great deal to be said for your arguments, but don't you think it would be a good idea if . . ." Stating her position hesi-

tantly, interrogatively, and above all sensibly, she sometimes manages to elicit a "Yes" or a "Maybe" from someone who a moment before had seemed in immutable
opposition. This might be called the mother technique. A
State Department career man, after watching her artfully
maneuver her way through a delicate discussion, once mur-
mured, "Never have I seen naiveté and cunning so grace-
fully blended."[3]

Then the psychologist sat with me through three
successive meetings of the big committee. We focused
on the interchanges which followed critical comments.
We watched the seven department heads especially.
When any of the teachers differed with one of them,
using "a shy, Socratic approach," what did he do? How
much resistance did he reveal?

Readers will realize that our observations could give
something less than meticulous indications. Instead of
a sharp meter-reading, we had only the crudest kind of
report. The two of us differed markedly on the characterization of 30 percent of the responses. We saw eye
to eye on 50 percent. We were apart only on the degree of resistance on the remainder.

The best conclusion we could agree on was this:
The soft approach makes some difference about two-
thirds of the time. In other words, if half the members
of a group will systematically make the effort to disagree with the others using some prefatory mollifying
comment, then six out of ten times the reply will ap-

[3] E. J. Kahn, "Profiles," *The New Yorker*, June 12, 1948, p. 33.

pear to consider the criticism without showing offense or signs of defensiveness.

This procedure was repeated with four other groups. The prevention scores were 45 percent, 50 percent, 60 percent, 75 percent.

From the point of view of good experimental procedure these results may well be considered irrelevant. Since no data are available on control groups there is no way of knowing whether these "findings" are accidental or unusual. Would the patient have recovered from his illness if he had taken no medicine?

Granting the methodological weaknesses and taking the quantitative conclusions with the utmost reserve, we do feel some confidence in advising participants in groups to think about their approach when disagreeing with others. If something like our recommended tactic is used without the positive results we obtained, then it should be disregarded without consideration for our findings. At the very least the effort may lead participants to consider the problem of defensiveness. At most the effort might evolve a better solution.

In passing, it should be noted that "the shy, gentle approach" fits the two explanatory theories. The gentle phrase doesn't stir up inferiority and it helps the speaker make explicit his attempt to criticize the argument rather than his opponent.

CHAPTER X

When Angry Look Again!

A lawn, a rabbit hutch, a much-loved rabbit hopping about free in the sun. Its owner, a little girl, has heard a noise that fills her with dismay. She rushes out to find that the terrier from next door has escaped into her garden . . . loud barkings, a horrifying scuffle. The inevitable is happening . . . she flings herself to the ground, for she cannot see that dreadful end.

Minutes pass, blackness, abysmal horror, when faintly a voice reaches her. "It's all right, Jennifer, the rabbit's safe." The child uncovers her face; slowly she approaches the hutch; no cry of joy; she turns away in contemplation. Five minutes later she is heard saying to herself . . .

"I must remember, always have a good look before you cry." —Innes H. Pease and Lucy H. Crocker, *The Peckham Experiment*, George Allen and Unwin, Ltd., 1943, p. 8.

"Make people a little less emotional, and you'll solve your discussion problems."

"Give me a group of men who won't let their emotions run away with them and we'll work anything out."

"There's nothing to this human relations but emotion. When you lick man's emotions, you'll lick his communication difficulties, too."

These are the more extreme examples of views expressed over and over by both leaders and participants. They were unsolicited diagnoses of *the* cause and cure of the discussion problem.

I tried on twenty-six occasions to pin them down. What do you mean by emotion or emotional response? What does a man do when he is emotional? In general, they had two things in mind: (1) behavior that was excited, agitated, or vehement, and (2) expressions of outrage, anger, irritation, or resentment.

I was struck, however, by something else in these interviews. These people talked about the emotion factor with overtones of gloom and defeat. Several threw up their hands in the traditional "what's the use?" gesture. "People are going to give way to their emotions and that's that." "When a man is in the grip of his emotions it's impossible to reason with him." "If a man gets emotional, and he's bound to if the subject is important and if his interests are involved, what good is it to try to persuade him to become problem-centered?"

This was the voice of futility. It was also the suggestion of an impossible objective. We were being forced to think about a phenomenon which was defined in terms which made dealing with it a waste of time. Our informants seemed to say that emotionality was inevitable and impossible to cope with, on the one hand, and then, on the other, that it had to be corrected if group operations were to be made efficient.

Is there a way out of this impasse?

We had some rough conclusions to start with. Excited talking was a sign of interest in what was happening. A direct attempt to make a man quiet down was not always successful. He often became angry at that. Is there any indirect way of persuading or forcing a man to soft-pedal or stop his expression of anger? We could not find one. We saw that an angry man disrupts a group. He refuses to listen. He makes others angry. People think about his anger rather than about the problem. Occasionally, we saw a man kid another out of his irritation. Sometimes irritation could be softened by another's expression of friendship. But most of the time an angry man was not to be side-tracked. He usually had his say, and his way, too.

We were almost ready to give up when once again we saw Jon Stone in action. It is ironical, but he helped us find a way out of our impasse.

His group was considering the draft of a statement of company policy. He was his usual antagonistic, arrogant self. As the clock ticked off the minutes he became even more so. But this time we thought he had a point. The rest of the members seemed unable to concentrate on the paper before them. They kept drifting off to other topics. His irritation mounted every time he tried to bring them back to the statement. And then we had it! We had been missing the point. It wasn't the anger, as such, we had to deal with, but the reason for the anger. Jon Stone's anger made sense. If there was justification for it why try to get rid of it? We had been looking at symptoms. Was there some infection behind the fever? The theoretical issue was now in the open. We had to deal not with every show of anger but only with those which were unjustified. Could those be dissolved?

A Point of View

What should a leader know about a man's emotionality and what should he do about it? A point of view which seemed to square with our understanding of the practical problem was worked out around the argument which follows.

Let us admit that a man is emotional. Let us also see that emotion is not something which merely comes and goes, but something that occurs *whenever* he is awake. He does more than feel, however. Alexis Carrel's insight is still a good one: "The man who thinks, observes and reasons, is, at the same time, happy or unhappy, disturbed or secure, stimulated or depressed by his appetites, his aversions, and his desires. The world, therefore, assumes a different visage, according to the affective and physiological states which are the moving background of consciousness during intellectual activity."[1] Feeling, in short, is not some occasional manifestation. It is there all the time. So is thinking.

We will not try to dodge Francis Bacon's assertion: "Numberless, in short, are the ways, and sometimes, imperceptible, in which the affections color and infect the understanding." An angry or frightened man will think differently from one who is amicable and secure.

Of course, emotions make a difference. But—have you ever wondered how the emotions come to be and when and why they become noticeable?

Consider this theory: A way of feeling goes with a way of thinking.

If you think something damaging is going to happen to you or those you love, and if you think you may not have the resources to ward off the damage, won't you feel fear and apprehension?

If you think that your well-being will continue or that danger is remote, and that your sources of strength are great enough to cope with danger if it should come nearer, won't you feel safe and confident?

If you think that what you are doing is important and useful and also appreciated, recognized, and adequately rewarded won't you feel interested, alert, enthusiastic?

If you think that someone is holding you up to ridicule, or is slighting or insulting you, or is making you "lose face," won't you feel angry, irritated, annoyed?

[1] *Man, the Unknown*, Harper & Brothers, 1935, pp. 126–127.

(Such an analysis could be made of all the other patterns of thinking that go with other patterns of feeling. Interested readers might well see how Aristotle analyzed the classic emotions in Book II of his *Rhetoric*.)

Feeling, in short, accompanies thinking. No thinking, no feeling. A certain mode of thinking, a certain mode of feeling. A kind of feeling, a kind of thinking.

Suddenly I encounter my old enemy. Anger surges up in me; I strike out at him murderously; he raises his right hand—and then I see that it has all its fingers. My enemy had two missing. Because my mind can go through a process of thought, . . . I realize that here is a case of mistaken identity. My desire to kill drops from me and becomes instead a desire to make amends, to help. The change in the direction of emotion has been brought about by thought. . . .[2]

Angell thought something. He then felt anger. He thought anew. He then felt apologetic.

What are we trying to do in discussion? Would we stop men from feeling angry, afraid, confident, interested? Not at all. We want only to have them look at "the man's hand." How many fingers does it have?

This is by no means easy, because an angry man is far more likely to look to his anger than to the situation which set him off. He doesn't do this because it is instinctive or natural but, we think, because he has rarely been told to do anything else. So we tell him to

[2] Norman Angell, *The Steep Places*, Harper & Brothers, 1947, p. 111.

do something else. "Stay angry—but look again at what you are responding to."

In our training classes we make a game of this. We deliberately try to persuade participants not to repress their anger but to add to it one thing more: *another look* at what they are angry at. "Stay angry," we say, "but look again, please, at the situation, the remark, the person. See if you are justified in being as angry as you are. Maybe the man has all his fingers."

This tactic is not designed to eliminate the anger, but to get the angry man to see if he has a sound basis for being so. If A purposefully insults B and B knows that it was done on purpose, B's anger makes sense. But if B merely surmises something in A's behavior, another look might change the direction of his thinking and his angry feeling.

The most interesting result of this point of view is that we now believe that three times out of four a man becomes angry because he thinks he knows his enemy when in fact he doesn't. So often the presumed enemy has all his fingers. In twenty-seven discussion interchanges in which one of the participants seemed angry, follow-up interviews with both revealed that nineteen contained elements in which someone became angry at his believing that he knew something that wasn't so. He was in those cases making assumptions about the situation. He was acting as if he knew when in fact he did not know. His anger was grounded on a guess.

The instruction was considered successful when a

leader (and others) could be moved to say, "Now, B, before you really get going, how about looking to see if he has all his fingers."

When they grew weary of the Angell anecdote we told them one about Blackie:

Quick-tempered John Stuart Blackie, the celebrated Scottish professor, was unusually irritable at the opening of a college term.

"Show your paper!" he commanded as the applicants for admission lined up at his desk. One lad held his a mite awkwardly and Prof. Blackie bellowed: "You little chap there, hold your paper properly. Not in your left hand, you loon, in your right!"

The boy muttered something, but did not shift his paper.

"The right hand, you loon!"

Trembling and pale, the boy lifted his right arm, revealing a burned stump.

The other students in the line howled and hissed at the irascible teacher, but Blackie had already jumped down from the platform to fling a strong arm about the boy's shoulder.

"Eh, laddie, forgive me," said the gruff professor, fighting back tears of remorse. "I did not know, laddie."

He turned a suffering face on the other boys. "I thank God He has given me gentlemen to teach—who call me to account when I go astray," he said.

Three dozen boys grasped his hand. It was the most successful year in the great teacher's entire life.[3]

[3] The Rev. Philip Jerome Cleveland, "A Man of Class." Reprinted from October, 1947, Coronet, p. 45. Copyright, 1947, by Esquire, Inc.

CHAPTER XI

On a Certain Kind of Excitement and Wonder

One main factor in the upward trend of animal life has been the power of wandering. Perhaps this is why the armour-plated monsters fared badly. They could not wander. Animals wander into new conditions. They have to adapt themselves or die. Mankind has wandered from the trees to the plains, from the plains to the seacoast, from climate to climate, from continent to continent, and from habit of life to habit of life. When man ceases to wander, he will cease to ascend in the scale of being. Physical wandering is still important, but greater still is the power of man's spiritual adventures—adventures of thought, adventures of passionate feeling, adventures of aesthetic experience. —A. H. Whitehead, *Science and the Modern World*, The New American Library of World Literature, 1949, p. 207.

Have you ever been with people who were so stimulated by their talking together that they hated to stop?

In the 200 groups I have notes on, that happened sixteen times. They were memorable occasions.

A decibel machine might have given indications of the quantity of sound in the room but it could hardly catch the quality of the eagerness and interest in what was going on.

I wanted to know how the participants explained the phenomenon. I talked privately with most of them after four of these sessions. These people had a sense of adventure, of going beyond the usual. If I gave a verbatim report of what they said I should give a skewed picture of what they were trying to say. I should be leaving out their excitement and wonder.

The Leader's Behavior

Several participants pointed to the behavior of the leader, which seemed significant to me, too. We need much more study of his type to know what he did. Now we can catalogue only a few negative factors on which there was much agreement.

In nearly every case the leader made no effort to push the thinking of the people in any one direction. One did not feel that it was necessary to satisfy him, that there were things he wanted to hear or views he didn't like. He never gave the least sign that he knew *the* answer. He did little to regulate or monitor the course of the talk beyond making his own contribution. He was no menacing, threatening outsider. Always he was one of the group working with the others.

They never had the uncomfortable feeling that they were in the presence of a critic looking for mistakes. There was no reason to be on guard because there was no guardian.

His attitude was one of effortless patience. Almost everything he did reflected the unspoken opinion that "If I do not interfere they will find resources in themselves." One sensed (because he never said it) his thorough confidence in them as persons who would find direction if no one inhibited their trying. His was no paternalistic benevolence, no shepherding of his flock. He was no father image on whom they could lean or to whom they would look for support. He was very much like that legendary French teacher whose criticism of his pupils' paintings consisted entirely of the confidential whisper, *"Continuez! Continuez!"*

A Member's Attitude and Manner

The leader was but half of the equation. Something came *from* the group, too. Members were so engrossed in what they were saying and hearing that they didn't see themselves. The observers, however, saw something which hitherto had been blurred. It was a distinction between a man's manner of speaking and his attitude toward problems.

Look first at the *manner*. It ranged between the two poles of *earnestness* and *half-heartedness*.

A person in earnest seems to believe what he says . . . thinks it important to have his say . . . has a strong desire to communicate . . . speaks with some force and volume . . . makes an effort to reach his listeners . . . shows an overall tension . . . gestures firmly . . . speaks with a rush.

The half-hearted person doesn't seem to care whether he makes his point or not . . . suggests an indecision and inconclusiveness . . . has no sharp sense of direction . . . reveals some disinterest . . . doesn't try very hard . . . is likely to look away from his hearers . . . pauses during his talk . . . is for the most part quiet and hesitant.

A man's speaking manner could be charted with considerable agreement by a number of observers on this sort of scale:

1	2	3	4	5
He tries hard. He wants to be heard and believed.	He speaks with some warmth and directness.	He shows occasional moments of tension.	He is lukewarm, hesitant, and indecisive.	He has a general air of not caring and not trying.

We had more trouble getting to the *attitude*. Hardly the least of our difficulties is the fact that most of the terms we should like to use have associations which are not relevant for our purposes. Nevertheless, speakers ranged from the *reasonable* to the *arbitrary* in their attitudes toward the subject matter under discussion.

When the reasonable attitude is in evidence the person shows that he has convictions but is still willing to listen. He has beliefs and conclusions but he recognizes that they may have to be modified if new data are presented. He has a theory and a proposal but he is willing to face the possibility that an alternative may be more useful. He is willing to ask with Galileo, "Who will set bounds to man's understanding? Who can assure us that everything that can be known in the world is known already?" His basic premise is patterned on Cassius J. Keyser's: "Actual knowledge is one thing; always imperfect and incomplete; but the spirit of knowledge is quite another, always insatiable and intolerant of limitation. . . ." He has a point of view but since he recognizes that it may not be all-embracing he is ready to reconsider it at all times. He understands the attitude of the men at the Institute for Advanced Study that Dr. Walter Stewart told about: "The young physicists . . . are beyond all doubt the noisiest, rowdiest, most active and most intellectually alert group we have here. For them the world changes every week and they are simply delighted by it. A few days ago I asked one of them, as they came bursting out of a seminar, 'How did it go?' 'Wonderful!' he said. 'Everything we knew about physics last week isn't true!' "[1]

At the other pole is the attitude of the arbitrary person, the man with settled opinions and fixed ideas. He has convictions and conclusions which may not be tampered with . . . he has spoken and why speak fur-

[1] Lincoln Barnett, "J. Robert Oppenheimer," *Life*, October 10, 1945, p. 136.

ther? He is like that editor who telegraphed the reporter: "Go out to Dayton. Get the truth about this flying story. Put an end to this Wright hoax. We know Men cannot fly." He is like that spokesman for a church group who bluntly told a 1948 conference: "We knew what we believed before we came here. These talks haven't changed our beliefs. Even if you prove we're wrong, which I don't think you can do, we'll still leave believing the same things we did when we came in the door."[2] Nathaniel Hawthorne has well characterized our man in the *Snow Image:* "But, after all, there is no teaching anything to wise men of good Mr. Lindsey's stamp. They know everything,—oh, to be sure!—everything that has been, and everything that is, and everything that, by any future possibility, can be. And should some phenomenon of nature or providence transcend their system, they will not recognize it, even if it comes to pass under their very noses."

These attitudes can also be put on a scale.

1	2	3	4	5
He has views which he will change in the face of data or larger views.	He faces the facts however uncongenial and takes some steps to incorporate them into a new position.	He admits a point now and then.	He is reluctant to consider data or views different from his.	He says or implies that what he knows or wants is "all" there is to it.

[2] *The New York Times,* September 11, 1948, p. 13.

Manner and attitude go together but they can be studied separately. Suppose that we are looking at ten people around a table and after an hour's talk we rate the bulk of the speaking at 4–5 on each scale. If our experience is germane, I should predict an impasse so long as this attitude and manner persist. And for the sake of simplicity suppose that members of another group were gauged at 1–2 after an hour's observation. I should predict progress rather than deadlock if this attitude and manner were to continue.

The governing factor was not the vigor or placidity of the manner but the degree of intransigence reflected by the air of know-it-all-ness. With five or six hours of practice we have been able to get a team of observers to a fairly high degree of agreement in spotting the degree of "allness."[3]

In nine (of the sixteen memorable) discussions in which this was studied, the observers' scores converged on the left.

The Achievements of Man and Men

It was in these groups that we saw the purest examples of the difference between a solo and a team performance.

History can be written in terms of the exploits of a

[3] For further analysis of this formulation see Alfred Korzybski, Science and Sanity, An Introduction to Non-Aristotelian Systems and General Semantics, Institute of General Semantics, 3rd ed., 1948, chap. 29.

Caesar, Napoleon, Lincoln, Roosevelt. Issues can be dramatized in terms of John L. Lewis, Joseph Stalin, Winston Churchill. Sports writers headline the winning pitcher and the scoring back. Congressional measures are remembered by the names of the sponsors.

But what serves as a useful journalistic device or a mechanical convenience often leads to obstructive modes of action in a meeting. In this vein individuals think and talk like soloists. They perform. They talk as if to preserve their featured positions. They argue against any view which would submerge their contributions. The fight for top billing among the stars of the movies is a reflex of their struggle for status. One may be amused at such goings on, but when it happens in a group something valuable is lost.

In the sixteen groups there was little evidence of the star system. There was a tacit understanding that a problem had been assigned not to this or that man but to all the men. They felt that their success would be measured by how well they picked all the brains in the room. It didn't occur to them to criticize what any one man said because they were centered on what the group could accomplish. These groups behaved as if they had been oriented in the mood of the famous Board of Consultants to the State Department Committee on Atomic Energy: "We agreed that all questions coming up were to be considered as being brought up by the group as a whole rather than by any member. If a member had an objection to any point, it was to be regarded as something that troubled the group as a whole."[4]

We heard very little talking which even hinted that another member was inadequate or unwise in saying what he did. Questions took the form, "How will that square with this? Is that what the rest of us are thinking? Doesn't that meet the difficulty?" There was no meek acceptance of what anyone said, but rather a full-fledged desire to analyze it as something the interplay of the group helped bring out. As one man said, "We've got to look at Joe's idea because if we hadn't come together Joe might not have had it."

How to Make a Difference

Up to this point it was fun to write this chapter. In a way what we saw in "The Sixteen" was the model, the goal of group deliberation. This is what we want more of. This is what Alexander Meiklejohn was writing about when he said: "Now the method of peace in resolving contradictions . . . is one of joint inquiry, of mutual helpfulness. When men are thinking together in peace each says, 'I cannot hold as true beyond question any opinion which my friend finds reason to question.' Facing a common problem, men think together, as well as independently. In such an

[4] Norman Cousins and Thomas K. Finletter, "A Beginning for Sanity," *The Saturday Review of Literature*, June 15, 1946, p. 9.

inquiry, evidence is not 'mine,' it is 'ours.' "[5] How do we go about getting this? Here the fun stops.

Our knowledge is incomplete. Nothing we tried gave us more than an approximation. We worked from the three factors: the non-regulating leader, the non-all-knowing attitude, the non-solo performance. We took leaders and helped them practice the non-monitoring role. That did something. We had the members of some groups chart one another on the arbitrariness scale. The more often they did that the greater was the shift to the left. Progress, though definite, was very slow. We have had groups talk over the solo problem and that helped.

But so far no group we have worked with achieved the degree of spontaneity and selflessness of the best of the sixteen. Perhaps they didn't have enough time to learn these "new" ways. It may be that our overly direct techniques of instruction were not the most efficient. We may have missed some factor in the group's operations more influential than those here described. There is reason to believe that we may have introduced a self-consciousness factor into the scene. A few of the more astute leaders thought we might have unwittingly made the people so sensitive to the process that it was diverting energy and attention from the effort itself. But in spite of the fact that we never once created anything equal to the sixteen by our emphasis

[5] *What Does America Mean?* W. W. Norton & Company, 1935, pp. 170–171.

on the monitoring, arbitrariness, and solo factors, it is clear that when the members of any organization look to them they will have an image of the goal they must reach. Given that, there may even be a change in what happens in succeeding sessions. At least this can be said: Whenever we worked toward that we saw a difference.

CHAPTER XII

Tired Leaders

Out of all the ways of waste there is none so vicious as that of your clever politician trying to run a business concern without having any notion of self-organization. One of them who took over Munitions for a time had so little idea of organizing his own energy that he nearly died of overwork *through holding up the work of others*; i.e., by delegating responsibility coupled with *direct access to himself* to seventeen sub chiefs. —Sir Ian Hamilton, *The Soul and Body of an Army*, Arnold, 1921, p. 225.

Only six times in all my conversations with leaders about the business of discussion was it said directly. But I thought many more intimated it. Or talked around it.

They begrudged the amount of effort it took to get people to talk and think together. They were unhappy about the value received from the energy they spent waiting for people to come to terms with each other. Was the nervous strain worth it?

When fatigue was joined with impatience it added up to discouragement.

This was the feeling that led so many of them to try to settle things themselves. "Instead of letting a bunch of men wear me down, I'd be better off working it out myself" is the way they might have said it if they had been given a cue. "It is easier for me to tell them what to do than to sit with them while we go round and round making up our minds" is the silent and accompanying refrain.

This is the state of mind which produces "little dictators."

It is also the attitude which stifles coöperative endeavor, which smothers initiative in staff men, which makes their bright ideas go into hiding, and which so overwhelms the chief that he cannot possibly get around to all the things which clamor for his decision.

It is also the reason why the chief gets more difficult to talk to, why he seems to listen with only half an ear. A man so bogged down with responsibilities cannot take kindly to a visitor about to add one more.

This in rough outline is a clinical picture of the man who has lost confidence in the values of human communion and who is but a step from a loss of confidence in himself.

I am undoubtedly on dangerous ground with this sort of sweeping conclusion but, with some discounting, it may be serviceable: The man whose weariness with the group process is manifest is also the man who is producing the conditions for his own insecurity.

Where is the man who can run a lodge, battalion, household, office, college—or any other organization all by himself? Where is the paragon who can see all things from his desk? Where is the godlike creature who can have all the creative insight?

It might be difficult to find a man who fits these specifications. It is easier to find men who act as if they do.

Why do they act so? What is there in the thinking of a man which lets him cut himself off from sources of strength outside of himself, which drives him to want to go it alone? Every important school of psychology has some answer. The Freudians, Adlerians, Jungians, behaviorists, Gestaltists, functionalists, etc. —each has a way of accounting for it. Readers would be enriched if they were to explore these points of view for understanding and guidance. It is no form of criticism if those views are omitted here. Nor is it implied that they could not offer counsel sufficient to deal with what is involved. This writer can justify an analysis of another view on but one ground: he found it useful.

This other view asserts that a man's unwillingness to work things out with other people is related to his assumption or unstated premise that for the most part phenomena are additive rather than non-additive. This view also says that the trouble is to be located in his failure to perceive the emergent, interactive character of facts.

What does this mean?

Sometimes things add up simply.

You have 109 books. You buy another. You have 110.

In your garden are seventeen rosebushes. A neighbor gives you some cuttings. In time you have twenty rosebushes.

You are out for a walk. You cover twenty-six blocks. You wish to visit a friend two blocks beyond. You walk twenty-eight blocks.

You eat two olives before dinner. You like them. You eat two more.

These are "plus" phenomena. Something is added to something else. The end result shows no sharp change. The number is greater in a small way. The effect is noticeable but not vividly so. There is a difference but no change in the pattern.

Sometimes, however, when things are brought together they do not just add up.

A cake of ice "plus" a handful of salt equals a pool of water.

From the union of a sperm and an ovum there emerges a different entity.

An atom of mercury "minus" one proton is no longer mercury but an atom of gold.

A husband and a wife who have a child have not just added to, they have complicated, their lives.

One cat "plus" one combative dog equals one fight.

These are non-additive phenomena. A thing interacts with another. Something new emerges from the interaction of the two. There is a dramatic development. The "plus" has become a dynamic complication. These things do not line up simply. They react, recreate, reciprocate.

The words "plus," "and," "added to" fit the simpler combinings. They do not map the complexities as well. There is no word in everyday use in English by which one can make explicit the dramatic character of these.

There ought to be a word which parallels the "plus" so that one could say "a husband and wife ———— a mother-in-law and father-in-law under one roof" and show that he understands the non-additive character of the relationship. Our folklore suggests that this is an eventful interaction.

That we have no such word suggests that we have not been overly sensitized to the character of these drastic combinings. One predicts that a word will be found or coined as soon as people start looking closely at these non-additive relationships. In turn the availability of such a word will call attention to the thing. For the present, however, it may be enough to face up to Leopold Infeld's question in his Quest: "If you saw two shops both proclaiming 'we sell fresh eggs' and you found by experience that one of the shops sold bad eggs and the other fresh eggs, would you still claim that the two shops are alike because they have the same sign?"

But what has this non-additivity to do with the job of the leader?

I wish here to draw on the work of Alfred Korzybski,[1] who made a generalized application of some findings of V. A. Graicunas[2] on the problem of "relationships in organization."

These findings have to do with the way an executive's burden increases with an increase in (1) the number of his subordinates or (2) the number of functions he is to perform.

A man has one assistant (or job). He "adds" another. He "adds" one more. He "adds" still another. He has four. Are his involvements and responsibilities now equal to four also? It would seem so if one assumes that things merely add up.

Some do and some don't. At a speed of twenty miles per hour a car can stop in roughly forty feet. At thirty miles per hour it takes twice as many feet to stop. But increase the speed two and one-half times to fifty miles and the stopping distance is increased five

[1] "Some Non-Aristotelian Data on Efficiency for Human Adjustment," Appendix IV, in Manhood of Humanity, The International Non-Aristotelian Library Publishing Company, 2nd ed., 1951.

[2] "Relationship in Organization," in Papers on the Science of Administration, edited by Luther Gulick and L. Urwick, Institute of Public Administration, 1937, pp. 183–187.

times, to about 200 feet. The addition is on an intensified scale.

With one assistant Graicunas describes one basic relationship. With two assistants the relations shoot up to six. The back-and-forth interactions of the three people have to be counted. The presence of the second assistant did that. "Add" now a third assistant and the back-and-forth, each-to-each involvements mount to eighteen. A 33⅓ percent increase in help is followed by a 300 percent increase in the demands on the executive's attention. He now has to face the influence of many more interconnections between and among his staff and himself. What any one does must be figured in terms of how the others will be affected. "Add" a fifth assistant and the relations skyrocket to 100.

But let's get back to our "tired" leader. He starts by being impatient with the slow working together of many minds. He says, "I'll do it myself." Neglect for a moment the possibility that he thus loses the experience and fresh vision of his helpers. He has "added" one more function. Or is it a third- or fourth-order complication? Or is it a drain on his energy, supervision, and responsibility quite disproportionate to the task—which he does not see because he assumes it is "just a simple addition"? He is then a man carrying a heavier load even though his perceiving apparatus hasn't caught it. He has become a man whose desk is unaccountably loaded, who hasn't the time to listen or talk.

In short, the pressure of non-additive factors builds up whether or not one sees the complication. It would seem, therefore, to be an exercise of wisdom to shunt off those factors wherever one can. What might soon become intolerable for one man might well be possible for more than one. A difficulty delegated may be a complication diverted.

This is not to deplore man's weakness. It is more an attempt at a realistic assessment and conservation of his strength, an attempt to keep him from buckling before the imponderably burdensome.

What applies to a leader applies to a group, too. A sampling of the items on the agenda proposed for thirty-two meetings made all too evident the general unawareness of the notion that things are not always simple. Give a group too much to do and, no matter how interested they are, they are in danger of bogging down in the doing.

Let a group be faced meeting after meeting with big, new problems before they have cleared up the old ones and it will not be surprising if they become tired. "Human beings are only human" is so palpably demonstrable that one is appalled at the number of occasions when human beings behave as if they were something more.

There would be little to be concerned about if fatigue were the only result. But people thus affected lose heart in the discussion process as such. Not seeing the non-additive weighting in the situation they look for a scapegoat. They see that their progress does not match their exertions. Therefore, the easy but irrelevant conclusion—do away with discussion.

I have talked about this with many leaders and in a number of instances they fall back on the "gold-bricking" explanation. "Staff members aren't interested enough. They're not willing to work hard enough" is the theme. I have not been able to check back in enough places to be able to say with safety that this is not a sufficient accounting. This could explain why more is not accomplished. But in the organizations I have looked at, the charge of "gold-bricking" was a libel. The men and women did not appear to be trying to get out of anything. They would not have been where they were if the desire to get out of work had been deep.

I might, of course, have been deluded. I might not have seen what the boss could see.

Nevertheless, I wish to urge a recognition of the possibility that the laziness theory may cover up the facts of non-additivity. At least these facts did not in my experience get the explicit attention they might have received. And, at the very least, if a group is given too much to do it is easy to test the hypothesis that either shorter agendas or more meetings would accomplish what is now unfinished.

Quite apart from any attractiveness (or lack thereof) one sees in this view, it had the merit of suggesting something to do.

First, we encouraged groups to give some attention to "agenda business." At the outset they would run down the list of items or problems, asking these questions: What can we deal with in the time we have today? What is the maximum we can tackle adequately? Never mind the sum of all we have to do—what can we do in this session?

In the beginning of our work with groups this seemed to be little more than a preventive device, a way of making explicit the dangers involved in a non-discriminative piling-on of non-additive jobs. But as we continued we found ourselves noting a very real emergent phenomenon—the people in the groups were realizing the need for more time to do what had to be done. They became defenders of the necessity of patience. This was not one of those dramatic changes, but a slowly developing awareness that there is more to the group process than meets the unobserving eye.

I cannot report that the increase in meeting time was inevitably followed by an increase in the number of problems solved. Occasionally that happened. More often the effect was a marginal and qualitative one— and one we had to make assumptions about.

A group which was protected against overloading seemed more relaxed, less under pressure. They seemed more disposed to listen. Their explorations were wider. Imaginative proposals had a chance to evolve. The leader especially seemed less harried, less impatient with the slow pushing and pulling of diverse nervous systems. He seemed to resign himself to the necessity of delegating rather than holding on to responsibilities.

These qualitative differences may well be products of the observer's imaginings. We were unable to reduce what we assumed to any measurable descriptions. As a matter of fact, by the time we came to realize what had happened it was too late to get the data. That there is something less than rigor in this kind of report is appreciated. This is where research is needed.

In the second place, awareness of the fact of non-additivity led to an analysis of the thing called a "solution." When is a problem solved? To ask that question is to realize that a "solution" is not some unitary entity but a word used to refer to a variety of creations. Here are a few kinds of solutions.

$Solution_1$ does away with the symptoms but preserves the difficulty.

$Solution_2$ corrects some aspects but makes new difficulties.

$Solution_3$ postpones the difficulty for a while.

$Solution_4$ eliminates a minor disturbance but touches the major one only slightly.

$Solution_5$ corrects one or two aspects of a situation.

$Solution_6$ deals partially with all that is apparent.

$Solution_7$ deals with the problem so that the sources of the major aspects of it are partially corrected.

$Solution_8$ deals with the problem so that the sources of the major aspects of it are corrected.

Solution₉ deals with the problem so that it does not arise
again and so that side difficulties do not arise
either.

If the reader will fill in the other possibilities we can
quickly get to say that a "solution" may be (a) of little effectiveness, (b) an approximation of a full solution, (c) a full correction. This makes inevitable, even
if something less than startling, our finding that (c) is
harder to achieve than (b), which in turn takes more
work, brains, and good will than (a). It hardly seems
necessary, also, to make much of the point that everyone wants (c), no one wants (a), and often (b) is the
best that can be achieved.

I must now venture another overly bread conclusion: that when you find a "tired leader" you will find
a man who wants nothing less than (c). The leader
who tends to be impatient of time spent is (as we have
seen it) also the one who is rarely satisfied with approximate solutions. He would pay for hamburger but
he expects pheasant.

When impatience is joined to the effort to achieve
perfection the result is again one of those drastic addi-
tions that multiply burdens.

How should leaders be advised? This has been a
stumbling block. Should we urge them to search for
approximate solutions? So few leaders are happy with
this half-a-loaf. They show impatience at our tempo-
rizing and weakness. "We're supposed to solve prob-

lems, not jab at them" reflects the attitude. Should we urge leaders to realize that big objectives demand big efforts? That takes us to more and longer meetings. Can a company, army, or any organization afford that? We face that question in the next chapter. For the immediate question we propose the following: A "tired leader" is something few organizations can really afford. The prevention of his fatigue is worth much. A clear facing of the facts of non-additivity really costs less than his impatience and discourage-ment. It is also less painful for those around him.

CHAPTER XIII

A Matter of Dollars and Cents

It is easy to make quick generalizations, especially when one is traveling. My Sicilian journal was crammed with neat paragraphs that reached hard and fast conclusions. It was a pleasure to write them, and at first reading they sounded very logical; some of them even seemed brilliant. By the second reading many of them had developed an acute case of anemia. And by the time I was ready to leave Sicily, nine out of ten had disintegrated into pretty but empty phrases. Among the few generalizations that remained intact was that it is foolish to generalize too freely about a people as old and as complex as the Sicilians. —Jerre Mangione, *Reunion in Sicily*, Houghton Mifflin Company, 1950, p. 245.

The president of Goods, Inc., was serious. "If I had the courage I'd dispense with a lot of our meetings. They take too much valuable time. Do you know what it costs this company to call a conference of department heads? Too much! Look at some figures. The twelve get a combined yearly salary of $500,000 . Suppose they meet once a week for two hours throughout the year. Figure it out. Fifty-two weeks times forty hours a week equals 2,080 man-hours times twelve men equals 24,960 total hours. That means each man's hour is worth about $20. That means it costs this company about $25,000 a year to run these meetings—or almost enough to hire one more good man." *

The president was still serious. "If you can guarantee to show us how to cover the agenda in half the time it now takes, I'll hire somebody and pay him $12,500 to take the load off someone else. I'll give you the other half. Then next year I'll hire a second assistant."

If this much time-saving could be promised and delivered, writing about it would hardly be justified.

Furthermore, even if it could be done, there is reason to believe that it would not be well advised. If the observations recorded in these pages mean anything, then a *saving of time as such is not an important or wise objective*. I believe this in spite of the fact that six out of every ten persons interviewed put "cutting the time of the sessions" as one of the most desired outcomes of improvement in the discussion process.

This belief was not easily reached. Most of the two hundred groups we observed were made up of busy people. Whether they were undergraduates or air or naval officers, business executives or housewives—they knew the tyranny of the clock. There was always so

*These figures have been updated to more nearly reflect salaries of 1980.

much else to do. Often another meeting had to be attended, or unfinished work was waiting.

Let me get to my point via a distinction between time-wasted and time-spent.

By time-wasted I mean the time taken up with the varieties of talking which keep a group from problems and solutions. This includes

- Any of the forms of misunderstanding which lead people to talk past each other;
- Any of the conflicts between people which lead away from a problem;
- Any idiosyncrasies such as a man's repeating himself, taking too long to get to his point, or elaborating on some pet irrelevant idea.

Whatever a leader or member can do to eliminate these nonproductive excursions is all to the good. Every minute spent in preventing or minimizing them is an attack on an unnecessary extravagance. These we would do away with. Much of our work with leaders, the case method, etc., about half of this book, is concerned with such time-wasting.

Unfortunately, however, this zeal for temporal efficiency carries over to a phase of the discussion process where it is not economical. That is, we have seen people who tried to save time when they should have been earnestly spending it.

I see this whenever men get impatient with the effort to understand complexity and the hard work of ironing out opposing views. I see it when men are willing to settle for some easy answer in order to get done with the talk. I see it whenever a man tries to wrap up a big difficulty in a small package. It is a spurious efficiency that saves time now only to spend it later. It is, indeed, no saving of time to push a problem underground today only to have it erupt another day.

Too many seem driven by the image of a vending machine. Put a coin in, push a plunger, pick up the package. Give me your problem, wait a moment while I turn it over, here's your answer. That's the way to do a problem in addition or to call something up from memory. It is no way to see one's way around a complicated situation to a solution whose effects may ramify through an organization. That takes time.

A woman who had seen one of the new giant computers click out an answer in a matter of seconds said it gave her an acute feeling of incompetence. It would take her days to get the same answer. Let her stop being haunted by this ghost of her own making. Can that computer work out a way of dealing with the unemployment problem that may come when it does the work of many men? That problem will take a creativeness which has not yet been built into a machine. That one will take time and infinite reflection. She might remember, too, that men were driven to make the machine to free themselves of the drudgery of computing so that more time would be available for the really important tasks.

Too many are moved by the unspoken assumption

that a man should be able to think creatively with the
same ease with which he decides to order pie rather
than ice cream for dessert. It is platitudinous in the extreme to say that small questions take small effort. But
how easy it is to forget the reverse. How easy it is to
get impatient when the big questions plague us. How
easy it is to fail to see that big problems are big. How
nice it would be if we could find some magic by which
to exorcise the bigness. How shall we acquire the patience to deliberate until we come to understanding?

There is no magic answer to that question either. It
may help just a bit to materialize the images, to face
up to the ghosts which haunt us.

The president of Goods, Inc., sat through this explanation without interrupting me. But I had another
point.

Now that you have heard my reasons for not wishing
to do the task you set for me, I should like to have you
consider whether or not you spend enough time and
money on meetings. Instead of cutting down on these
costs, may I ask you to think about adding to them. It
is rather easy for you to compute the cost of a meeting
in dollars and cents. You talk about a meeting as if it
were something like a dead charge on your operations.
But is it that necessarily? Isn't there equal cogency in
looking at the hours you all spend in talking together
as a fundamental feature of your operational effort?
Men don't just act. They act in terms of plans for some
ends, good or bad, efficient or inefficient, explicit or

inexplicit in varying degrees. Is not the careful definition of what is to be done an integral and inseparable
part of the doing itself? Could an organization evolve
procedures without working them out?

The president appeared impatient for the first time.
I was, perhaps, belaboring the obvious. But he let me
finish.

I have listened in on enough meetings to realize that
the absence of communication between men costs
money and makes trouble. Indeed, we are just beginning to realize the economic significance of questions
like these: How many problems come up because
somebody didn't take the time to tell those around
him what he knew that they should have known, too?
How often unwittingly does an employee or a staff
man bungle a job because some manager or officer
somewhere didn't get time to explain what was
wanted? What happens in the hurry of the day when
a man doesn't feel like breaking the silence to ask for
information? These are not new questions. They
merely give point to the argument. When there isn't
enough communication in an organization, look for an
emphasis on temporal efficiency. Look for that devil
notion, the search for a spurious simplicity. It could be
that I am merely enlarging on the story of the traveler
who said, "Indians walk in single file." "How do you
know that?" he was asked. "The one I saw did," he
replied.

The president of Goods, Inc., ended the conversation.

"What you say sounds good as you say it. There is no doubt that we ought to talk together even more than we do. But we're so busy producing and shipping goods we have no time for talk. If we talked as much as we should who'd do our work?"

Well, let me have the last didactic word. It takes more than a pair of hands to push over a big tree. The roots of our beliefs about temporal efficiency go deep. Men who have been trained to think in terms of cash per hour are not easily persuaded to extend that view. Where is the cost accountant who can figure the factors in the human spirit? Who knows how to calculate the comforts which come when men understand each other? Or, perhaps, I am resaying what Francis Bacon took account of in his essay "Of Dispatch."

Affected dispatch is one of the most dangerous things to business that can be: it is like that which the physicians call predigestion, or hasty digestion, which is sure to fill the body full of crudities, and secret seeds of diseases; therefore, measure not dispatch by the time of sitting, but by the advancement of the business; and as in races it is not the large stride, or high lift, that makes the speed, so in business, the keeping close to the matter, and not talking of it too much at once, procureth dispatch. It is the care of some, only to come off speedily for the time, or to continue some false periods of business, because they may seem men of dispatch; but it is one thing to abbreviate by contracting, another by cutting off; and business so handled at several sittings or meetings goeth commonly backward and forward in an unsteady manner. I knew a wise man that had it for a byword, when he saw men hasten to a conclusion, "Stay a little, that we may make an end the sooner." On the other side, true dispatch is a rich thing; for time is the measure of business, as money is of wares; and business is bought at a dear hand where there is small dispatch.

CHAPTER XIV

On Preserving Human Warmth

We talk for a thousand reasons. We talk to transact business, to find our way, to gain the importance that comes from being the first to carry bad tidings, to ferret out the news of our friends and tell them ours, to express sympathy or receive it, to advertise our operations, to salute the weather, to indulge in gossip, personal or political, or to repeat a joke. Mainly, however, we talk from the deep-seated, age-old human need to talk. That is one reason why some people, even when they are alone, can be heard mumbling away to themselves, sadly bereft of listeners but happily free therefore of the fear of interruption.
—John Mason Brown, "Conversation Piece," *The Saturday Review of Literature*, February 19, 1949, p. 24.

It will come as something less than a surprise to those interested in committee activity to read once more that the leader plays an important part.

Nevertheless, from the very beginning, our observations either started with or ultimately returned to him (or her). I am now almost ready to say that if you let me look through a peephole so that I can see and hear only what the leader is doing and saying, I can predict (within limits) how the discussion is going. I can tell you little about the actual content of the argument but I am willing to venture some conclusions about the range of participation, whether the problem is being attacked or dodged, how much conflict there is, and whether joint solutions are emerging. This is really less a matter of skill than of experience in charting the leader's actions.

We have notes on 143 leaders. It is hardly necessary to believe that these findings would be duplicated by observers who met with a similar number elsewhere. The findings may not be representative. I report them, despite that possibility, because they lead to some practical and specific advice.

Though each of these leaders was an individual with his own blend of characteristics, six types came into focus. Readers will understand that the simplicity of this analysis was belied often by the complexity of the persons. This is a listing which is more convenient than precise. Even so, I did see individuals who fitted one of these classifications more than another.

1. *The Director* (77). He is the man who makes the arrangements, defines the order of business, has opinions about how the issues are to be decided. He functions very much like an orchestra leader, movie director, or

puppet master. He runs things. He tells people what to do. He has a sense of failure and disappointment when things don't go according to his plan. When a session is unproductive his analysis of it rarely includes his role.

2. *The Councilor* (24). He is the appointed head but he considers himself not above but in the group. He works with others in planning the business. He has conclusions and suggestions but he presents them as a participant rather than as one with the privileges of position. He assumes that he is a member of the council whose organizational assignments are additional, not superior. He is quite willing to share the blame whenever the work is unfinished.

3. *The Parliamentarian* (12). He is the man with the "Rules of Order" at his elbow. He wants proposals presented in the form of resolutions and motions. He likes to recognize those who wish to speak. He doesn't try to impose his problems or solutions, nor does he seek to censor those he dislikes. His emphasis is on decorum and legislative nicety. Orderliness is more important than relevance. He will hold up the discussion of new business, though the group is eager to get at it, until he gets through the formality of announcing that the old has been completed.

4. *The Quiet One* (9). He believes that his function begins and ends when he (a) opens the meeting and (b) declares it adjourned. Talk has a way of eddying and flowing around him. He does little to push it along or slow it down. He is willing to serve because for him custom is stronger than purpose. He sits placidly and

patiently. Honored at his election to the chair, he rarely feels the necessity for further service. He refers questions to the secretary. When someone insists, he will appoint a subcommittee, though he prefers volunteers.

5. *The Good Host* (10). He brings good will to the party. He calls people by their first names. Problems to be solved, issues to be clarified—these must be disposed of quickly. Sometimes he plays the genial tyrant "fixing things" so they don't come up. Conflicts are not to be thrashed out so much as laughed away. He has an anec' dote for every contingency and when he doesn't he invites one. He nods readily whenever he hears a point made on a note of optimism. "Aw, what the hell . . ." is the sign that he is about to deny a difficulty.

6. *The Chief Clerk* (11). He is the meticulous guardian of the group's virtue. He knows how things came to be and is careful to parade that history when issues are in danger of being redefined. He feels responsible for the preservation of procedural rigor. He is less interested in working things out than in seeing that they are worked out in "the right way." He would rather work on the by-laws than on problems. He worries about details. It isn't enough that the members evolve policy. They must also state procedure so clearly that their assistants know easily how to implement the policy.

This listing was made after my visits with the first 100 groups. Since there were so many more Directors than any other type I was moved to interview each one encountered in the remaining forty-three leaders.

There were twenty-seven. Twenty-four were able to stay for a period after the business meeting.

The interviews were informal and organized around some twenty questions. Relevant here are the first two: Do you think that the discussion you just led was (1) an effective and (2) a satisfying one? If not, what factors would you have liked to correct or eliminate?

From the replies it is possible to construct a composite picture of what these Directors consider a good discussion.

1. The people should deal with the business on hand with no digressions and no dealing with subjects not on the agenda.

2. There should be no time wasted by speakers "beating about the bush" or repeating themselves.

3. Everybody should listen carefully to everybody else.

4. The required decisions should be reached and all plans made.

5. The less bickering the better.

6. The chairman will keep things moving in orderly fashion from point to point.

7. Several people will not try to talk at once.

8. The floor is not to be hogged by a few. Everybody is to have an equal chance to speak.

9. No long speeches.

10. People should know what they're talking about, and not talk when they don't have a worth-while contribution.

11. No interruptions.

12. Everybody should arrive on time and stay until the end of the meeting.

13. Dispense with preliminaries, like announcements, reports, and gossip and get down to business.

This composite picture confirmed an impression: that the Directors were interested in the "effective" but not the "satisfying" part of the question. I pressed the point each time. They were not interested in making the talk-experience anything more than a time of work.

They were missing something.

They were too mechanically-minded. They wanted people to perform like gears and wheels in fine balance. They would have preferred people who were freed of their interests as individuals. They wanted the discussion to proceed as if it were a military maneuver on the parade ground. People were somehow supposed to divest themselves of every interest but one.

Well, people are not puppets. Men can be made to follow the script in a play. They can also make a play up as they go along. "Creative Dramatics" in the schools is fascinating evidence of the way students can be encouraged to discover their potentialities.

When men are driven they lose spontaneity and the zestful interest in what goes on. They seem to be more around the business than in it. The sense of personal concern is lost. They are present, but not in what happens.

There is a very real danger that our concern with improving human communication may lead members of groups to forget the human part of the matter. This topic was put near the end of this book on purpose. If the objectives of the previous chapters are achieved at the cost of human warmth we shall have bought unwisely. We need efficiency *and* satisfyingness. One may try to rig a discussion in the image of a belt line; if he succeeds he may find that those who attend become as inert as machines without the capacity (or will) to create.

These Directors had little sense of any need to make the discussion a pleasant as well as a productive experience. They seemed to forget that men find pleasure in just talking together without regard for outcome. What is the purpose of conversations at luncheons, dinners, teas, cocktail parties, chance meetings, reunions, smokers—to solve problems or to facilitate the exchange of friendly feelings?

A meeting is a place where one can be heard. And it may be that it is more important for a man to say something than that he be badgered into sticking to the point. We shall be doing something to ease the pressure on a man's insides if we give him time to talk it off. The point may by no stretch of our imagination be related to the point a man makes, but to him *the* point is the one he is making. Let a Director forget that and he is in danger of losing part of his audience.

In some of the most satisfying discussions I have watched there was a continuous alternation of mood. The members swung between the serious and the playful, the relevant and the remote, kidding each other and laughing at the problem, with thrusts at the problem and inexplicable asides.

The zeal of the business-only Director in such a session was happily impotent in the presence of forces deeper than those he sought to tap. Sometimes by his very persistence he was able to turn his men from their very human interactions to his robotized endeavor. He thought he was getting things done. He was; but he was undoing something, too.

In our training sessions with such Directors we urged them (especially when the going was slow) to make a joke. We were rarely successful in showing them how. We are resigned to the belief that there may be no way to build a sense of humor in a dedicated man.

We are content with one accomplishment. It is a small one but we are persuaded that its effects radiate far. We have been able to get some of these Directors to sit back, to listen with lessened tension when the bent to comedy or diversion or personal release is being manifested. His job is not to prevent it, but to pick up the problem *after* the camaraderie or tension has been spent. He is to think of himself as the conductor of an orchestra in a rehearsal, letting his men play at will during a break and then after it urging them to look to the music.

There is a small danger in this conception. The conductor wants no fooling around during the reading of the music. But for us improvisation during the discussion may be the most expedient way of getting ready for concerted action. A jam session in the midst of the program may help us stay in tune when we get to the score itself.

CHAPTER XV

The Reminder

"Men should be taught as if you taught them not,
And things proposed as things forgot."
    —Alexander Pope, "An Essay on Criticism."

One of our most valuable developments was the role of the Reminder. Whenever we found something worth trying with a group we were faced with the question of approach. Should we work on the leader or on the group or both? Should we take time to lecture the group on what they were doing and what they should do? Should we put our instructions in the form of a memorandum which they could read outside the meeting?

It was neither practical nor possible to get a busy staff, board, or committee to take much time off to think about their discussion techniques. Now and then they might give me a few minutes but more than that seemed to disturb them. I had no trouble interviewing them individually before and after, but somehow I was in the way once they met as a group. This was an invitation to despair. How could communication in a group be dealt with if they wouldn't let us tell them about it?

At many points we had to work on and through the leader. But it soon became clear that he was being given too many balls to juggle. He needed help. It was suggested that we get a man from the group to do our work en route. Why not teach him what we knew so that he could undertake the reëducational effort as an "added duty"?

One other conclusion was forced on us—that a great deal (perhaps all?) of our advice (though fundamental) was rather elementary, that little of it was outside the experience and knowledge of men and women important enough to be able to participate in planning conferences. The task was not so much to tell them what they didn't know as it was to encourage them to apply what they did know. Or as Dr. Johnson put it, "It is not sufficiently considered that men require more often to be reminded than to be informed."

In the face of this it seemed wise to find someone in the group, other than the chairman, who would remind his colleagues whenever they were moving unproductively.

It took much trying and fumbling before this man's job was defined. He seemed ever to be doing something more than was desired. The more we studied him the more it became necessary to restrict his activity. When he misunderstood his job he simply became one more road block in the group's progress.

The restrictions took this form.

1. You are not to act the umpire calling the verbal plays. You are never to play critic, revealing mistakes or telling anyone that he is "wrong."

2. You are not to act as an adviser, telling the group that they should do this rather than that. You are not to assume the role of expert-consultant brought in to make decisions.

3. In the language of the military you neither have authority nor command responsibility. You must do nothing to deny the obligations for action that belong to the group. Your voice is to have only the importance which you as a member of the group possess.

The instructions took this form.

1. You are to think of yourself as an aide or administrative assistant to the group. Just as a script-girl makes a record of action in movie-making so you are to note from minute to minute the details and overall pattern of what goes on. You are a kind of observer for the staff with your eyes and ears fixed not so much on the matters under consideration as on what members are doing in connection with them.

2. The substance of the previous chapters is to serve as a check list of what you are to look for.

Is someone misunderstanding another's words, items, or assumptions?

Are they too solution-minded?

Are they getting to the problem?

Are they suspicious of compromise?

Are they in the experience-innocence muddle? Would the presentation of a case help?

Is a stigma word stopping discussion?

Does the problem belong to the group?

Would it be wise to remember the value of the alternation of mood?

Are they racing through the business?

Is the agenda too long?

Etc.

3. Suppose, for example, someone in the group has contradicted someone else, and as you listen to both assertions and replies you think one is referring to items not in the catch-all statements of the other. Suppose, further, that you believe this interchange is likely to continue without the speakers' coming to see what they are doing. Then, and only then, do you get into the discussion.

What do you do? You

a. ask a question about the procedure

b. in a dead-pan manner.

You ask, "Is it possible that Mr. Asserter has in mind some items which are different from those Mr. Replier had in mind?" or "Mr. Asserter, are you and Mr. Replier talking about the same items or details?" or "Gentlemen, are you both referring to the same things?" The way you phrase the question is not as important as that you ask a question. This is designed to keep you from becoming a contestant. If you state outright, "Mr. Asserter, you are not talking in Mr. Replier's terms," then you open the situation up for another contradiction. But ask a question and that possibility is averted.

You are not to put the question so as to imply your own answer. You can turn to Mr. Replier and act as if you knew that he is focusing on different details. This, too, makes you a contestant. You are to say your piece in your most neutral or dead-pan manner as if you were wondering whether, rather than telling him that, something is amiss.

It is not easy to convey in print the difference between a question (1) as it might be asked by an aggressive prosecuting attorney and (2) as you should put it. The difference is a matter not only of tonal emphasis and force but also of mood. You are to speak quietly, colorlessly. You are to have no overtones of accusation or suspicion or superior wisdom in your voice. When you speak as instructed you are more likely to invite consideration of the mechanism of misunderstanding than a defensive reply by those involved. Just hint that you know they are misunderstanding each other and you become a target. And your reminder value to the group has diminished.

The Value of the Reminder

This dead-pan-question tactic gets results far out of proportion to its intrinsic significance. It is like oil on a dry bearing. In my experience when the Reminder learns how to use it as a means of getting at the sources of breakdown in discussion rather interesting things happen. In three staffs we saw this result: Within half a dozen meetings after our Reminder began to function others took to asking his sort of question about what was happening. His mode of approach was contagious. These groups achieved an insight into what they were doing that we should not have predicted.

So valuable is the role of the Reminder that I am quite willing to go this far: A group cannot achieve its maximum efficiency in deliberation without one.

A batter is so intent on his effort to hit the ball that he really cannot see how or what he is doing. An outsider, a coach, can often detect something in the swing that the player is wholly unaware of. People around a table give so much energy to the business at hand that they see only it and not their approach to it and each other. An outsider's eyes may be no keener but he can direct them to things the participant misses.

The training of a Reminder is a rather simple (though not necessarily a sure-fire) affair. He is taken through the material of this book in leisurely fashion. He is shown what to look for. He meets with a tutor after both attend "real" meetings for a review of what happened. He is urged to try out his spotting of the procedures on the tutor. He practices the neutral manner on the tutor. He then tries his questions on his group.

After about eight hours of such instruction with a tutor, the people we have worked with are set out on their own. In seven out of ten cases the instruction takes in varying degrees. The failure with the three we attribute to our own tutorial inadequacy and to something in their orientations which makes them prefer to participate in rather than observe and question the character of the goings on.

The major objection to the use of the Reminder is that the group in effect has lost a man. If he has a post of any importance his interests in the agenda may be lost. His department may suffer. There is no answer to this from the point of view of group functioning. When this objection was raised in one staff we were able to train the department head's assistant. He was invited to the staff meetings with the usual privileges of voting, etc. But this was a makeshift. The department head was an excellent Reminder. What he did had noticeable effects. Our hope is that as men gain experience in these "new" ways of talking together they will be able to take turns reminding and participating. When each can perform both roles we should rise above so much of the stress we now know.

CHAPTER XVI

The Image of Men
Talking Together

About twenty years ago in the final pages of *The Epic of America* James Truslow Adams said that "The American Dream" was best exemplified in the Library of Congress. It came "straight from the heart of democracy, as it has been taken to it." It was for him "a symbol of what democracy can accomplish on its behalf." He was struck by its efficiency and service, "the generous aid of Congress," the private gifts, the four million books and pamphlets, the devotion of the director and staff. Adams' feeling for this symbol went one step farther, to the people who came there.

As one looks down on the general reading room, which alone contains ten thousand volumes which may be read without even the asking, one sees the seats filled with silent readers, old and young, rich and poor, black and white, the executive and the laborer, the general and the private, the noted scholar and the schoolboy, all reading at their own library provided by their own democracy. It has always seemed to me to be a perfect working out in a concrete example of the American dream—the means provided by the accumulated resources of the people themselves, a public intelligent enough to use them, and men of high distinction, themselves a part of the great democracy, devoting themselves to the good of the whole, uncloistered.

It seems to me that it can be only in some such way, carried out in all departments of our national life, that the American dream can be wrought into an abiding reality. . . .[1]

I read those words when the book was first published. I now appreciate the spirit which animated them even though I should apply them to an institution somewhat humbler, more evanescent, certainly less heroic in organization—any group of men and women who meet to talk together in committee. There is drama there, too. The image of men talking together is not without its own grandeur.

That committees fumble and fritter away good time is no original discovery. But that men can make the effort to come to terms with each other is a dream that goes beyond the boundaries of America. This is possible to all men.

It is, moreover, peculiarly the heart of what Pendleton Herring has called "the politics of democracy": "The faith of democracy, for all its shibboleths and

[1] James Truslow Adams, *The Epic of America*, Little, Brown and Company, 1931, "The Epilogue."

hypocrisies, is still based on the fundamental tenet that society can continue peacefully even though men agree to disagree. Out of this attitude we may be able to make the continuing adjustments to each other and to our environment that are inevitable in any social process but which have seldom been accomplished in the past through methods short of violence."[2]

The lesson of our experience is that we must not sit by and expect a faith in democracy to evolve by itself into democratic forms of action. Men and women do not come to attitudes of mutuality simply by living. If we have learned anything from observing committees at work it is that people can stand some coaching in the arts of talking together. Attitudes of patience, respect, and understanding which are so necessary to group functioning require encouragement. The environment in which men talk can be designed with the achievement of these arts and attitudes as the significant objective. We need not let their development arise by chance. We can proceed to their realization.

[2] Pendleton Herring, *The Politics of Democracy*, W. W. Norton & Company, 1940, pp. 432–433.

Index

75 76 77 78 79 80   12 11 10 9